Advance Praise

"This talented first-time author has captured the journey of healing and self-discovery in a way that hasn't been done before. *Courage to Rise* reaches out of the pages, grabs you by the heart and soul, and makes you believe—and by that last page, you feel like someone *really does* understand."

—**Kimberly Kirberger, New York Times Bestselling Author of**
Chicken Soup for the Teenage Soul

THE LIFE LETTERS
Courage to Rise

THE LIFE LETTERS

Courage to Rise

Emma Grace

NEW YORK

LONDON • NASHVILLE • MELBOURNE • VANCOUVER

THE LIFE LETTERS
Book 1. *Courage to Rise*

Published in New York, New York, by Morgan James Publishing. Morgan James is a trademark of Morgan James, LLC. www.MorganJamesPublishing.com

The Morgan James Speakers Group can bring authors to your live event. For more information or to book an event visit The Morgan James Speakers Group at www.TheMorganJamesSpeakersGroup.com.

All photos courtesy of Unsplash.com and Pixabay.com, released under Creative Commons CC0.

ISBN 9781642790030 paperback
ISBN 9781642790047 eBook
Library of Congress Control Number: 2018936433

Cover Design by:
Rachel Lopez
www.r2cdesign.com

Interior Design by:
Christopher Kirk
www.GFSstudio.com

In an effort to support local communities, raise awareness and funds, Morgan James Publishing donates a percentage of all book sales for the life of each book to Habitat for Humanity Peninsula and Greater Williamsburg.

Get involved today! Visit
www.MorganJamesBuilds.com

for the one beautiful heart who has never stopped
believing in mine. my mother.

Note From The Author

This book is for the believers and the dreamers. The ones who still have their starry eyes and hopeful souls. Who chase after big dreams and have big hearts and still believe in big love. This book is for the ones who fight for what they want. And keep their hearts whole no matter how many times they get broken. For the brave hearts. The ones who willingly, trustingly, and without fear, still place a beating heart in someone else's hands. To hold. To nurture. To love. This is for you.

For the strong women we know and raise and love—and mostly, *are*. May you know a lifetime of happiness. And during your journey, may your greatest love story be the one you discover within your own heart. *Yours.*

with love

Maybe you're sitting there, wondering how you got to this place. Maybe you're going over and over the things you wish you hadn't done—and all the things you have. Maybe you're picking apart that last conversation. Wondering what you could have said or done differently to change how things turned out. Maybe you go over and over that last day. That last moment. Wishing you could change something—anything. Wishing you could take it back. Or get them back. Darling, hear these words like they are being written just for you: *you are going to be ok*. And all that stuff you're analyzing? You can't change that. No matter how sad it makes you. No matter how much you regret it. No matter how much you wish you could go back and do it again. So you need to do something for you. As hard as it's going to be. And as impossible as it's going to feel. You need to take that first step. Now. And you need to let that go. *Let it go*. It's ok if it doesn't make sense yet. It's ok if you have some loose ends. It's ok if you have to forgive someone that isn't even sorry. And darling? It's ok to forgive yourself, too. You did the best you could at the time. Stop beating yourself up. You are not broken. Things are not hopeless. This life is going to be a good one. I so totally promise you that. And this part? This is not *all* there is. Oh no, darling. And there *are* more amazing things coming than you'll ever know. So take that with you. Tuck it away. Rest easy with it as you fall asleep. This is not your end, sweet soul. This part? This hard part? *This* is your beginning.

draft
after
draft
she had sketched
her life.

some parts
in pencil,
others
in **permanent** ink.

it was the
job of a lifetime.

this single
canvas.

this *one*
masterpiece.

One day you'll get it, sweet girl. You will. You'll understand that it's not always your fault. And you will learn to stop telling yourself that. When people don't treat you well. Or love you. Or believe in you. You will learn that those things are *not about you*. So many of us are carrying around that burden—that belief that what happens to us is all personal. We start believing that we are a reflection of the people who don't—can't—love us. And we're not. So please, please, please hear this, sweet girl. Hear it. And then make it part of you. You are beautiful. You are exactly, precisely, and perfectly created to be the person you are. Complete with the dreams dancing around in your soul. And the passion propelling your heart forward. But you are also put on this earth and made to bump into thousands of hearts along the way. Some that will walk with you. Others that will push you. Some that will break you. And others that will heal you. But each and every one is part of your journey, and they make you who you were meant to be. See them for what they are, darling—without using them as your mirror. It's not your fault when a relationship breaks. Or love fails. Or people walk away. Whether you knew someone for two days or two decades—it always, always, takes two willing hearts. And so you can have the best, most wonderful, giving soul in all the world—and that won't be enough if someone doesn't meet you halfway. And that's the lesson, sweet girl. It's not your fault. Protect your heart. Make it believe this truth. Someone is out there looking everywhere for you. Dreaming of you. And one day, they are going to measure their entire life by the day your eyes met theirs. So until then, be confident. Be strong. And keep that heart full of more hope than fear.

darling,
please
please
please
stop thinking
this is
all your fault.

Never again would she want something that looked good to the world but wasn't right in her own heart. It took her a few hard-earned scars to get to this place. But she did. And now it was totally, absolutely, amazingly clear. Despite what they told her, it was never about what the world wanted for her. It wasn't even what the people who loved her—whom she loved—wanted for her. It was about what she wanted for herself. And it was as simple as that. She had been with the hearts who looked good in the photos—the smiling, happy, sandy beachy ones. She'd worn the clothes and worked the jobs and surrounded herself with the experiences that the world pushed on her. Told her were important. That were part of the *good life*. But her heart was still unsettled. It was trying to love the picture of life she was painting for it—but it couldn't. And she knew it. In the depths of her heart and soul, it whispered. *Find your life, sweet girl. Find your heart.* And that's how she knew. Happiness—her happiness—was never going to be found in the voices of the world. The ones that shouted at her. Compared her. Told her who and how and what she needed to be. She'd never be able to catch up to all the world's spinning and tilting and shifting—and the chase would just end up leaving her empty. And I guess that's when she got it. The single most important lesson she has ever learned. What the world thought? That was none of her damn business. And from this point on, she was going to chase the things that made her whole. And fulfilled her. The things that were real. She wanted what made her eyes sparkle and her heart melt. She wanted to give—love, and time, and understanding. And she wanted to be loved. And understood. So she was going to spend her life chasing those things. From this point forward, everything would be different. Everything.

she
spoke those

three little words

and **silence**
echoed back.

but they weren't
the wrong words.

just

the wrong ears.

And sometimes that's how you rise, sweet soul.

From the fire burning around you. From letting go of what has been holding you back. Weighing you down. Sometimes you have to trudge through the darkness, all alone, believing and hoping with every part of who you are that you're heading the right way. And sometimes you need to rise from the ashes. After losing everything you thought you needed and everyone you thought you should have. It's just how it works. Darling, your life is going to come together. I know it seems so hard—so wrong. But this is temporary. This is your time of challenge. Of darkness. The time you're being put through something—tested—because you're on your way to something so much greater. I need you to believe that. You have to trust that what is happening right now is not failure. It's not *I can't believe this is my life now* and *I'm too old for this* and *I've had my chance.* And no, this whole part—it's not your forever. No—so totally no. This is the part where you find out who you are, sweet girl. This is actually the best, most defining chapter in your whole story. And just wait—what comes next is going to make you believe. In fate. In timing. In love. In a greater plan. *I promise.*

They always told her that she was so strong. She never understood why. There had been things she'd experienced that had crushed her. And people she'd wanted so badly to hold onto—that had taken her heart with them when they tore away from her life. There was *so much* she didn't understand. About why or when or how things had happened. Or would happen. And for every part of the journey that she'd been called strong—she had felt weak. And vulnerable. And sad. She had cried. *Oh*, how she had cried. And maybe she had never believed them because the world had made her believe that strength meant untouchable. The people with the hearts that couldn't be hurt. The ones who wore the armor and protected themselves from anything and everything that could ever hurt them in this life. But she had lived long enough now to understand that was *not* what strength was. Strength didn't come from not breaking—from letting nothing in—letting nothing threaten a kind of love she'd do anything to protect. Because that wasn't living. And now, what she finally realizes is that those people who had called her strong? *They were right.* She was strong. Not because she was untouchable—but because she was unbreakable. She knew that *no heart* escaped without bumps and bruises and scars and loss. Without whispering those three little words once—with all the hope and faith and courage in the world—and hearing silence echo back. So yes. Loving means chances and risk and every single damn thing in between sometimes. If you do it right. But the strong ones—the survivors—they fall and learn to walk again. Every single time. Stitching the pieces of their hearts together as they go. Even if it must be on broken feet.

close your eyes.
imagine
    the person
you loved first.

    was it you?
ok, then i guess
we have
some work to do.

The world was a tough place. And for a while there, she felt like that was all she saw. Caught up in this all-too-crazy race—she felt like she was always competing and fighting and chasing for *a little more this* or *a little less that.* And I guess you could say that she got really, really tired. The world kept taking and taking. And she was down to counting the hours in the day—looking at the equation and trying to see what else could fit into the time she was given. It was a heavy burden—always feeling like it was her against everyone else. Living in a world that told her constantly that she didn't measure up. And when she started to realize that she had been judging her progress and her value by someone else's measuring stick—it made sense. All that chaos and competition was changing her. And she didn't like it. So one day, she just woke up and took herself out of the race. This was about her. And what was right for her life. She finally realized that if she's constantly comparing—then she really isn't being true to her own heart. And that is what mattered. *What really mattered.* So she slowed down. And got to know herself. She took all the things off the list that the world had made important—and she reprioritized the real things. The things she was drawn to. That made her feel alive. And you know, that simple decision changed it all. Because when she started to love who she was and where she was—she didn't feel like she was so caught in the swirl of this crazy life. Trying to be everything. With peace on the inside, she learned, nothing that knocked on the door could hurt her.

It's not wrong. To love someone. Darling, it is never, never wrong. There can be wrong circumstances and wrong timing and wrong geography. Actually, there quite often is, isn't there? There can be hearts you shouldn't love or shouldn't have loved as long as you did. There can be people who didn't deserve it and didn't deserve you. There can be love you can't explain with people you can't explain—and love that grows from parts of you that you didn't even know existed. It can be confusing and hard and wrong by a million other standards, sure. But that love that grows in your heart for another soul? That part no one else can ever really understand—that sometimes *you* can't even understand—*that* is real. It will always be real. Don't try to extinguish it because you shouldn't feel the way you do—or because you don't want to. It might not end up being your fairy tale, sweet soul. But anything that awakens that part of you—that opens your heart—is worthy of a little exploration. Let it in. And see what it grows. And darling, if you believe this is your fairy tale—you say those words out loud for the world to hear. You take the chance or the risk or the whatever you want to call it. Because you'll either get your blessing or your lesson. And you'll need them both. And you know, love can be right in your heart—you can love someone completely and totally—and it might not end up being their fairy tale. That's ok. That's the beauty of it all. It's a risk. But it's worth it. Because when you meet the right ears—the right heart—there won't be silence echoing back. There will be love. The kind that changes everything. The kind that is whole and real and true. The kind that meets you where you are, gently takes you by the hand, and shows you how much more is coming.

Let me tell you how it's going to be. After this.

Because I know you can't see it right now. I know you're in the middle of this crazy, confusing, tug-of-war. One that leaves you wanting to just fast-forward. Past the hurt. Past the questions. Past the heartbreak or loss or whatever it is you're walking through. So I'm going to help you *see*. Because what happens next—it's amazing. And I want to be sure you keep believing. I want you to know that there is an end to this chapter. So here it is.

After this, you are happy. Not because you have all the answers. Not because everything *makes perfect sense*. But because things *make more sense*. All that—it was progress. You went through a little bit of hell and you came out. You emerged with a few battle scars, a great story, and some strength that didn't exist before. And darling, you use it. You use it to shape your life into what you want it to be. You stopped being a passenger. You stopped letting other people decide what you want. You found your voice. After all this, you no longer let people mistake your kindness for weakness. You make sure people know what you think. And you find what you're looking for. Because you wouldn't give up. Because you wanted it so badly. The world slowed down its turning—its crazy spinning—and now you get to enjoy the ride. After this, you get to stand at the edge and look in all directions. Fully. Completely. You know what's behind you. And you accept it. For it made you what you are. You know what's beside you. In the here and now. And you enjoy it. Because you understand the immense and yet measured finality of time. And you dream. Because you know that is really what propels you forward. Hope. For a better tomorrow.

this
is
not
all
there is.

It was one of the most beautiful things she'd ever learned in this life, yet also one of the hardest things, too. Something that had both broken her and strengthened her at the exact same time. But she had learned how to do it—and she had learned it well. It was an art—how she had taught herself to be unafraid of being afraid. But it made complete sense to her—that art. She knew there were going to be times that didn't make any sense. When things were dark and the path was bumpy and she'd lose her way. She knew she could love something or someone with every shred of who she was—and in a moment, they could walk away. She knew she'd lose things and be lost. And she'd break hearts and be broken. She knew she'd stand at the precipice—more than a few times—knowing she'd have to grow her wings on the way down. And she'd be scared. She'd be fearful and wary and hesitant. And that was alright. Being afraid was alright. But she always promised herself—always—that she would *never be afraid to be afraid.* Because that's where change and potential and life lived—in those little pieces where she was pushed outside of what she knew. And who she knew. When life forced her to be different—to try something different. That's always when it happened. Because honestly, she would never be ready—to step forward, to let go—and that is why life constantly surprised her. That was the grand plan. There would be some unexpected. There would be some fear. And that was life. It was always going to be ok in the end—even if the middle got a little messy sometimes. She had faith in the process. And she would *never* be afraid of being afraid. Never.

Don't call her beautiful. I mean it. Don't say she has beautiful skin. Or eyes. Or hair. Just *don't*. Because that's not who she is. Her beauty is so much more than what you can see. Really. And trust me, you've never seen the kind of heart this girl has. She is a soft, sweet, honest soul dancing around in a hard, hard world. Yet somehow, she stays that way. Sweet. Loving. Full of faith. With an empathy for other hearts and an untouchable stubbornness about what's still possible. She is the kind of girl that recharges you. Makes you feel like you can still believe. Still find what you're looking for. And yes, she *is* beautiful. But not just in that simple way a photographer can capture. Her beauty springs forth from a well deep within her. And it always will. She's a light in a world of darkness. Fluorescent pink in a world of gray. She's the kind of soul that changes the world. So don't just call her beautiful. Call her *everything*.

She told you. Over and over. She told you she'd do it. That she'd get there. You told her it was impossible. That those things *just don't happen*. And she just smiled. Undeterred. And kept working and planning and hoping. You told her to focus on something else. So she worked harder. You told her *these* kinds of things just *didn't happen* to girls *like her*. So she dreamed bigger. And every single day—every single time she heard you say no—she refocused. She knew the universe fought the hardest against people who had the possibility to change it. So every time things got more difficult, she smiled. Because she knew she was getting there. And she was *going* to get there. In her heart, she couldn't blame them. Because they didn't know. They didn't know that it was love pushing her. And faith driving her. And they just couldn't yet see that she was born with wings. And this whole process—this was just her learning to fly. And she *would* fly. And those wings would carry her. Because she was the one in a million. And this was her destiny.

this
was the year
she learned
to love
herself.

Maybe it's pulling back a little. So you can think through what's going on. Maybe it's getting out there and being in the mix of it. In the loud, chaotic mess of life. Maybe you need to speak up. And tell them exactly what you want and how you feel. Or maybe you don't even know how you feel yet. And you need time to figure it out. But no matter what—*no matter how much* the world tries to push you and direct you and make you feel happy and pressured and sad and stressed and everything in between—don't you *ever* feel guilty. For doing what you need to do. For choosing what is best for you. Even if it means sometimes there are people who just won't get it. Who won't support you. And maybe, who won't be there standing next to you in the end. Because you know, sweet soul, sometimes *it is* just about you. Sometimes you've spent so much time doing what is right for other people, tending to their needs, and asking them what they want—that you forget you matter too. So whatever it is, do it. Do what is best for you. There will be some people who won't understand. But that's ok too. Because the right ones will. And they will be there, standing beside you. Cheering you on. Towards a stronger, happier, more confident version of yourself. And at some point soon, those people are going to see you for what feels like the first time. And they're going to smile. Because they get it. And you do too. It's not always about you. But this time it is. This time, you come first.

the
trick
is
you
teach yourself
to believe

in the
moments

it's hardest

to believe.

He broke your heart. Or she did. Or it did. I know.

You placed your trust and your hopes and your dreams in it. In them. With clear eyes, you took the very heart out of your own chest and you handed it to someone else. To hold. To protect. To nurture. And that made you vulnerable. It taught you the simplest and yet most complex part of living. How to love. How to be loved. How it is possible to love someone else—maybe more than yourself. How to see the best in them, even though you know they aren't perfect. You share secrets. And memories. And random, crazy, no-one-else-will-ever-get-it moments. You are everything to each other. And you truly want them to have everything they've ever wanted—even if it's not you. And then that cruel little irony of life creeps in and taps you on the shoulder. *It's not you.* And just like that, your heart needs to learn how to be whole again. How to find its way back to you. Intact. So you can use it to love yourself again. You want to pull back and hold back and lock it away. You don't want to feel that empty—that broken—ever again. But you know the truth, don't you? Love is life. You can't hide from it and you can't run from it. There are no promises and no certainties, and sometimes, there just aren't forevers. We are imperfect and changing and human. So things are going to end. You're going to break. But darling, love is *still* the purpose. Without it, life is empty. You are empty. So you pick that heart up and you piece it back together. And then you let someone else hold it. Completely. Totally. And without fear. Sure, there will be a lot of people who drop it along the way. But your heart is strong and courageous and made to be held. Love like crazy, darling. Love like crazy.

first
it hurts you.
then
it changes you.

There was a time she wasn't sure. In the middle of a hurricane, it always made her question. Wonder whether she was walking the right way—and whether the risk was worth it. She'd have those doubts. What if—what if what was ahead of her was *not better* than what was behind her? The should-haves and could-haves and if-onlys would dance through her head. Would cause her to slow—to stand still in the raging winds and torrential rains—and look around her. But it was funny, because that's where the truth always found her. Out in the open. In the middle of the storm. When she was most vulnerable. And maybe it was because her ears couldn't hear through the chaos of the storms that her heart could. And it whispered. It told her—and tells her still—to calm her fears. So she listens. Because she knows, even if she wanted to, that she can't go back. Life is a crazy, beautiful, confusing journey—but it is lived forward. So when those doubts and fears and questions dance through her head and threaten her feet—she has to decide. And she chooses to hold fast to hope. Because that's what carries us all. That little part of us that has the courage to let go and seek unknown boundaries and uncharted landscapes and boundless dreams. It becomes what propels us—and reminds us—of those simple answers. Simple truths. That you will find *that* again. That *you will* be happy again. And mostly, that things will *be ok again*. So keep moving, sweet soul. Let your heart carry you when your feet are tired. It knows where it's going. Always forward.

The day had come. Everything was different now. Before this moment, it had been more about what looked good to the world. She had worn the clothes. And surrounded herself with groups of smiling, happy, beautiful friends. She'd taken the vacations. Put her toes in the sand. She'd been with the hearts who had pretty faces. She thought—they thought—that she was living the good life. And maybe she was. But her heart wasn't full. She didn't want just a pretty face standing next to her—she wanted a *beautiful soul.* Who made her feel loved and wanted and whole. Who encouraged her dreams like their own. Who held her hand gently—and yet somehow encouraged her to walk on her own. She didn't want the circles of smiling friends that showed up for pictures and holidays and nights out. She wanted the close, special few who dropped everything when they heard the crack in her voice. Who knew the reason behind her smile. And her tears. She wanted the things that felt good in her heart. That fed her heart. And from this moment, those were the things she was going to chase. This was that before-and-after line she had always heard about. The one that separated her life into two halves—the one where she was living, and the other where she found out why. It finally made sense. Her heart was full—full of hope and potential and love. And she knew it—good enough was no longer going to be good enough anymore. *Now*, she wanted it all. And that girl with that heart? She was stubborn enough to get it.

good enough
was
no
longer
going to be
good enough
anymore.

She wondered why. So many times she had wondered why. *Why* was that question her heart always asked—always wanted to ask. It followed every ending. Every heartbreak. Every loose end. Her life—her heart—seemed to be stitched together with a million different whys. Why had things happened the way they did? Or didn't? Why did the timing feel so off—so different than what she had expected? There were so many questions. And so few answers. And the thing she had learned about questions was they hurt. They made her feel alone. Maybe it was because they compared her and measured her. Forced her to become the person who hadn't gotten what everyone else had gotten yet. The one who was always ahead or behind or faster or slower than where she should be. The whys filled her world. And then emptied it at the same time. They made her feel misunderstood. *Different.* Different, that is, until she decided to look at them differently. And the truth was, she was *always* going to have questions about this life. And how it unfolded. How timing and chance and opportunity painted her life in the colors it did. But truth? Her set of whys were what made her—her. They were what set her apart. She wasn't alone. Just because she seemed a little ahead or a little behind in the great race—she wasn't going to look at it that way anymore. She was going to see these times as an incredible opportunity. A chance to grow. New eyes and a stronger heart. These times of too many questions and very few answers? These were actually the most important ones in her life. Her big chance. For these were the times she had the opportunity to learn her own heart. So she set out on that journey. To find love with the only heart she was destined to be with for a lifetime. *Hers.*

it's
the end
of the beach,
darling.

or

it's the start
of the
ocean.

your call.

Perspective. The only thing that can change sadness into hope. Loss into a lesson. And an ending into a beginning. Perspective. The sweet, simple, and yet incredibly hard-to-obtain differentiator in this life. What separates those of us who will make it—from those of us who won't. When we see it in others, we call it positivity. Or hope. We call them unbreakable. We look on in awe while these people smile through every bit of what life throws their way. We watch how they look at each hardship as an opportunity. And somehow, push away negativity. And bitterness. And then we think these people *are born*. Born with that undying positivity. That unbreakable spirit. But the truth is—they are made. Just like we all can be made. By a conscious choice. That is repeated. Until it becomes part of you. One choice. To take what is happening—or what happened—and stop making it something that defines you. It's the decision to *limit* its power. To look grief or loss or betrayal straight in the eye. And say this *is not about you anymore*. That's when it happens. You choose to focus on squeezing the good out of every single damn thing. Everything. No matter how deeply it cut you—you look as long and hard as it takes. Until you can find it. The good in the situation. The laughter. The hope. The opportunity. Yes, I know—some will say this is naive or idealistic. Maybe. But since we can't choose what we get in this life—the best thing we can do is choose how we take it. And the first couple choices will be hard. Trying to find joy through tears—and pain—it's not natural. Yet. But it will be. Darling, focus on the life *you want*. Because it just may find you.

Darling, one day it's going to make perfect sense why it never worked out with anybody else. I know how it used to be. How it used to feel. You were the other half. You did everything together. You plus them. But now, suddenly, it's just you. You feel lost. Alone. Like something is constantly missing. And you want to go back, don't you, darling? Because the memories bombard you—at the most random, crazy times. And the ones that haunt you? They didn't really even mean that much while they happened. But those are the ones that get you. That hit you like a ton of bricks. It's funny, isn't it? How it's not the big moments you remember. It isn't the red-letter days that you spend months planning for. It's the everyday moments that haunt you when they're gone. The times when things were simple. When they were yours. And you were theirs. The Saturday mornings. The Tuesday dinners. The hugs after a long day. And you want to go back to when you were the half of another whole. Because that is what you miss. And that is what you know. But darling—the truth is going to heal your heart much faster than the remembering and the missing and the longing. You have to start over. From where you are—from this moment. And you need to redefine your life again. Your life—with *you* as the whole. Not the half. Because the truth is, as hard as it is to believe right now, this *had* to happen. For some reason, this was the end. And maybe it's just for a little while—and maybe it's forever—but no matter what, you have one and only one job right now. Pick yourself up, dust yourself off, and go find yourself again. Really. I'll bet you forgot who you are—and what you really wanted. It's easy to forget your own heart when you're holding someone else's. So do it, sweet soul. Find that you again. And let the one that is destined to be your someone find you there. As that girl. Happy. And whole. Dancing your heart out on life's dance floor.

she

is a
light.

a sweet
happy
soul

who
still
believes

in the
magic
of this
world.

let her dance.

She saw the potential. She believed in him and them and their future. She believed in who he *could* be—who he *wanted* to be—who he *almost* was. She was one of those rare hearts that somehow loved you just as you are—and yet made you want to *be* everything you weren't. She was a *once in a lifetime.* A *you're going to wait your whole life for this.* But he couldn't see it. Didn't see it. His heart wasn't open. And his eyes weren't ready. They would be, one day. He would look for that kind of love again—for her again. Because he would *finally* learn that a heart like that ruins you. In the absolute best way possible. He would see it one day—but much, much too late. He would look for her—towards her light. And for the first time, he would see that she was his rainbow. The color in his world. But by then, she would be gone. He'd find himself thinking of her often. Wondering how he missed it—and if one day, he'd ever find her again. But her? She would be off. Happy. Dancing through the universe. Lighting up the stars in someone else's sky.

She has a special kind of strength. The kind that was built over time. Slowly. Deliberately. She accepted long ago that the world wasn't always going to give back what she gave. And that was ok. Because she wasn't doing all this for something in return. She didn't care if it was reciprocated. Or celebrated. Or even noticed. She was doing this because it was what she chose. Oh, she knew there was evil. She chose good. She knew there was hate. But she chose love. She wasn't naive. She wasn't avoiding the truth. She was *curating* it. She was selecting and focusing on what she wanted in this life—and rejecting the rest. She was doing this because she had finally learned that life wasn't going to give her anything for free. It was up to her to make the kind of life she wanted to be part of. All of it. She would have to surround herself with the people that breathed life into her. And push kindness and patience and love out into a world she knew would often push nothing but the opposite back. But that's what her life was about. Standing strong against anything that threatened to break her.

And it's funny. Because she never set out wanting to change the world. But you know, I think that's exactly why she did.

She was never scared of love. Never. She knew full well she could find the soul she was meant to dance with on this earth—and still, there would be no promises of forever. Life—life didn't come with forevers. As much as she could love someone, and as much as they could love her back—tomorrow was never promised. And she knew it. So that girl just went out there and she loved. Without reservation. Without boundaries or regrets. And without promises. She knew tomorrow would come if it was meant to. For her, for them—for their two hearts standing as one. She was a believer in what was—and a hoper of what could be. She wasn't afraid to say how she felt. Love—as she saw it—was the most diverse, yet most beautifully complicated thing we had in this life. And she loved how it could change eyes and hearts and souls. How it could turn a hardened heart into a believer of soft words and sweet nothings and gentle brushes of the hand. It heals us and breaks us, hurts us and makes us—but it's always pushing us towards something that is real. Because the heart cannot lie, sweet soul. And it wants what it wants. And so that girl accepted the truth about love. It wasn't scary. She knew she could be broken—and she would be—but that was the gamble. And the odds were in her favor. Because she wanted to experience that kind of love. The kind that was real. And she was going to love like crazy. Because it was alright—all of it—as long as she steered clear of the one and only dangerous part of loving. The gap between what she said and didn't feel—and what she felt and didn't say. Because that—that—was the only place love could ever be lost. Everything else? That was just how the heart found what it wanted. By the imperfectly perfect art of loving.

you *deserve*
to be
someone's
best thing.
and chances are,
you are.

She dances into the lives of the hearts around her. Like a whisper. On tiptoes. It's like they don't even see her coming—and she just drifts in and changes everything. A little at a time, and yet somehow, all at once. She makes them believe again. In the future. In life. In themselves. She makes them hope and dream and see the world for what they so much want it to be. She's an invisible force. Moving things and rearranging pieces and putting the right things together. Like the wind. With the power and strength and ability to change absolutely everything. But she does need one thing.

That girl must stay free.

Oh, I know it didn't happen the way you wish it had. The way you wanted it to with every single beat of your heart. They wronged you. They hurt you. It wasn't fair or right or justified what they did. What happened. And you just want to *understand*, right? If only you just understood *why*. Then maybe you could move on. You could let it go. You could make peace with how it all went down. Right. All that is very true, except sometimes it's not going to happen like that, sweet soul. Sometimes you are not going to get the answers. So, you have to teach yourself the hardest, yet possibly the most important lesson you'll ever need to learn in your life—and no one else can do it for you. How to move on. Without answers. With so many questions. All the while, somehow forgiving someone who isn't even sorry. And may never be sorry. It's hard. But your time is so very precious. And if someone didn't treat your heart—your life—with the care a heart like yours deserves, then they have had enough of your time. Stop looking back at that chapter, sweet soul. It happened for a reason, and you're going to understand it completely one day. But until then, find your happy. Find your heart. Find your peace. And let that whole chapter be finished.

just promise
  you will never
touch anything
 with half
  of your heart.

Sure, she had said it. And she had thought it, too. Sometimes *this isn't fair* just crept in without warning. She had those times when she thought over and over that *she didn't deserve this* and *she had worked so hard to get here.* And she could admit that sometimes, she spent a little too long asking herself *why* things happened like they did. So yes, sometimes, she let those feelings creep in. The ones that made her feel sorry for herself. That painted her as a victim. But never long. Never did she let those feelings linger too long. Because she knew how it worked. The universe wasn't blessing her or punishing her. There was no fair or unfair. She wasn't guaranteed to get something just because she wanted it. Or had worked for it. Or because she had tried ten times harder and wanted it ten times more than someone else. No. If she wanted something, she was going to have to get out there and fight like crazy for it. Every single day. Until it was hers. She'd have to get up early. And stay up late. She'd have to be bent and broken and told no. She'd have to sacrifice and hear people tell her it was never going to work. And she'd have to keep going. In spite of all that. She'd have to be stronger than the people working against her. She'd have to fight harder than the rest of them. But mostly, she'd have to keep her eyes focused on *her* journey. She knew it was going to look like others had it easier. Got it easier. And maybe they would—but all that didn't matter. Her path was simple. One foot in front of the other. Every single day. Until she got where she was going. No matter what came at her—no matter what tried to break her or stop her or slow her—she knew the truth. Forward *was forward.*

hold on,
dear heart,

i am
fighting
my way
back
to you.

There will be storms. Sometimes you'll hear their rumble in the distance—you'll have time to prepare, to take cover. But others, they'll just sneak up behind you and catch you unready. Vulnerable. Alone—out there in the middle of some field. And that's perfectly alright. Because storms are going to come. And yes, some of them are going to last a long time. They are going to test your resolve and force you to stand strong against the driving rain and the punishing winds. But you know, darling—you're going to be ok. *You are.* When the storms come, you do your best to shield yourself from the chaos of the winds and rain. And you hang on like hell. You're never going to feel totally prepared. Ready to face the darkness and the power and the enormity of it all. So you just do what you can—you hear me? *Just what you can.* Remember that. The storms of our lives are a part of our story. Sometimes they'll last longer than we wish they would—and sometimes they'll take things with them we wish they hadn't. And as crazy and hard as it is to trust, we have to believe in these parts of our lives as much as the sunshine and blue skies. We need them. We need these times to refresh us. To remind us. To allow us to rebuild. So don't ever fear them, sweet girl. When you hear the rumble—and see the lightning flashing in the distance, you'll know. A new chapter is about to begin. Try to be excited about what is to come. And until then—hang on, darling. Hang on.

All around her, people were knocking. Asking her to let them in. They came with clothes *they thought* she'd look better in, magazines that showed her *a better* body, and promises of *all that could be.* If only she gave up just a little—just a little—of who she was in exchange. If she handed over a piece of her, she could become *that* much better. She could have the perfect relationship. The best body. The newest styles. She could be the one people flocked to. With the flawless skin and perfect teeth and long toned legs and whatever else she wanted. They came promising friendships and gifts and advice. Knocking. Loudly. Every single day of her life. And inside, she would peer out the window, watching them. Carrying their promises. And then she'd look around and discover a strange peace. She was content. And no part of her wanted to give up a piece of her heart to become who they thought she should be. She may not be perfect by their standards, but she had created a world where she was happy. With who she was. And what she had. And everything she actually wanted to be. She used to ignore them. But now she wants them to know that she doesn't need them. She doesn't want what makes her look perfect to the world but keeps her unhappy in her heart. She doesn't want the relationship that looks perfect in photos, and tears at her heart every night. She wants to *be* happy. And make others happy. So she doesn't need them. When the world knocks on her door—with all its empty magazine promises of happiness—she no longer answers. Because she knows where her happiness stems from. And it's not there. The world will not beat her. Because she knows when to open that door. And she knows exactly what she wants to let in when she does.

she
wanted

someone
who loved her

in the
same way
she had
finally learned

to love
herself.

maybe
it had
always been in her.
but one day,
she just
cast aside
her worries
and whispered
to the universe —
go head.
i trust you.

Every time she starts to lose hope, she catches herself. She pulls herself together, gets herself focused—and gives herself a pep talk. Her own *heart-to-heart*. And it's always part realistic part hopeful and part magic. She knows how she wants things to be. And she accepts how they are. But she knows there's a long road in between where she is and where she's going—and it's going to have some twists and turns. It's going to be paved in some parts—and in others she's going to just have to get out there and make her own way. Sometimes she compares her path with others. But she always catches herself. And she stops her heart from making it all some big competition. Because the truth is—this life is *hers*. And the timing of what she gets and *when* is only partly in her hands. And she's ok with that. Because she knows the best parts of life are the surprises. Especially the ones that come disguised as loss. Or heartbreak. The things that somehow twist her around to face what turn out to be the best things in her life. And sometimes, those surprises she could never have imagined are waiting in the *tomorrows* and the *next weeks* and the *just-hang-ons* of this life. So she's going to hope. And believe. That tomorrow—tomorrow—may be just the day she's been waiting for. The day that shows her exactly what she never knew she always wanted.

she
had changed.

and it
was both
**the decision
of a moment**

and the
journey

of her
lifetime.

She shouted at the world. And it shouted back. She fought and argued and pushed and led. She stood for things. And she stood *up* for things. She put her voice and her opinion out there. Every single day, she spoke her mind. Not because she necessarily wanted to make others believe what she did—but because she wanted to fight for what she believed was right and true and good. But every day she was out there shouting, someone else was shouting louder. And every time she got out there to fight a battle, someone else was starting a war. She was one voice against the world. One drop in the ocean. One ripple on the pond. And even still, she was never going to give up. Never. But she knew to keep the fight in her, she had to do things differently. Everyone could shout. Everyone could speak their mind. They could fight for a cause and put their minds on a poster. They could stop and start whole movements. But not her. Not anymore. She was going to try a new approach. A simple one. She was going to lead from the heart. *Her heart.* And she knew the heart was so powerful that volume didn't make one bit of difference. The heart had the power to change eyes and feet and lives and yes, other hearts, too. She could plant seeds—words and actions that would grow in others and have a thousand times the effect a voice could. She wasn't going to be just a voice on a line, a tee shirt in a crowd, a poster in a hand. No. She was going to change the world by her action, not just her opinion. She was going to get out there and be who she wanted—expected— hoped—to be. And one day the world would accept her—*embrace* her. Hell, maybe they'd even love her a little bit, too. But whether they did or didn't, that girl was going to walk heart-forward. And she knew it would take her so much further than she could ever imagine. And honestly, after that, she couldn't *wait* to get there.

You know, maybe it's time. For forgiveness. For that *thing* you've been holding on to. I know you've been waiting for a reason. So that you can understand—so you can make *sense* of it all. I know you wanted an apology. And wanted things to work out. But the trouble is, the longer you waited, the longer you waited, right? And maybe you thought you had time. But darling, you *don't*. And *they* don't. This life is a crazy, chaotic, beautiful ride—but it's short. And you don't know when you'll run out of chances. And here's the thing. None of us—none of us—are going to dance through this life having made no mistakes. We are all a little broken. A little lost. And maybe they meant it, maybe they didn't. Maybe you'll never know. But there are two things you need to remember. One—forgiveness isn't about them. It's about *you*. And two—people are imperfect. We all are. And sometimes we do things we can't explain. Things that hurt people. Maybe we mean them at the time and regret them later. Maybe we don't. Just know that sometimes it takes a lot longer for some people to get to that place where they can forgive. Where they can let go of the pride. The words. What was done. Or wasn't. But no matter what, please know this. Forgiveness is the only piece—the only *peace*—we control. And it's time. It's time to control your happiness again. And maybe your forgiveness will never find the ears of the forgiven—but your heart will know it. And darling, if you are lucky enough to have the opportunity to look someone in the eyes—to tell them, *with all sincerity*—that the past is the past? Do it, sweet soul. Your heart will give up some of that space it's been using for bitterness and anger and will make room for what you need most. Love.

there are
   exactly
three ways
   to love each other.
constantly,
      unconditionally,
and unfailingly.

One of the most important lessons she had ever learned was no. It was one of those she never knew she had to learn. And honestly, even when she did, hadn't wanted to. Because as one of the big ones, this one hurt. It came with a life-changing message, sure. But also—often toting heartbreak. And loss. And pain. It meant there were hands she had to let go of. And times she had to walk alone. It meant she had to struggle. And be tested and bruised and challenged. In these times, everyone told her to *just wait*. That *she'd understand one day.* Part of her always hoped that was true, but part also wondered whether that was just one of the things people said. *It's not.* It's completely, totally, amazingly true. She knows that now. For every single thing she has lost—every single thing—she has found understanding down the road. And acceptance. And strangely—yes, even love—for the way things happened. *Are happening.* The understanding usually came much later. But there was always a reason for the hurt. Always. Maybe because the timing was off or maybe it was because she needed to be redirected towards something different. Something better. Maybe it was simply because that thing or person or opportunity just wasn't right for her. And she didn't even know it yet. But what she did finally accept is that the universe wasn't holding her back. Nothing was working against her and she wasn't being punished. No. The *nos* and the *not right nows* were shaping her. Making her. Directing her. And what came next was always better. Maybe it wasn't immediate, but the good would come. So in the end, she's learned to look at life a little differently. She likes to hear *yes* and *here you go.* But maybe no is the real miracle.

sometimes,
when it rains,

i hear
the sun
whispering

wait.

She had been searching the world. And all the moments and people and interactions in it. She kept looking for the answers. The c*ertainty*. The *sign*. The things that told her she was making the *right* choices. Going in the *right* direction. Spending her time at the *right* job or school or choosing the *right* place to move. Whether she was loving—or would ever find—the *right* person. Her questions were many. But her answers were few. And so sometimes she spent so much time watching and thinking and analyzing, it just started to make her wonder. From the very depth of who she was, these questions plagued her. How would she know? When the right heart came along? Or the right opportunity? Or the right time to risk it all and just go for it? She tried to figure it all out. Map out the plan. What it should and would and could look like when all the pieces fit. But she got tired. And that's when the first big question was answered. One day, there was a sign. Like she'd waited for. From somewhere, she just felt the universe stop her in her tracks. From all her worrying and overthinking and analyzing. It whispered.

Darling—when it's right for you, you'll know. You will so totally and completely know. You won't be overthinking. You won't be searching. You won't be "trying to make it work." When the pieces fit, they just fit. And that's all there is to it. So learn to let go a little. Of trying to plan it all out. That has been done for you already. And soon enough, you'll know exactly what happens next. And why it had to be this way. Until then, sweet soul, how about you just learn to enjoy the ride.

**she decided
logic and reason
could only take her so far.
and then she'd just have
to get out there and
fight for the fairy tale.**

She knew what she wanted. She had always known. And it wasn't
the everyday kind of love. All around her, people were finding their
someone. And settling down. But she was out there, still looking.
Their reasons were many. *It worked. It made sense. They'd been
together forever.* But her reasons were different. She didn't want just
the everyday kind of love. She wanted the inspirational kind. That
had sparks and butterflies and love and strength. Where they could
somehow both be themselves and yet better people all at the same
time. Some told her to settle. That there was no such thing as fairy
tales. Well, maybe that was true. For them. But she knew we each had
our own idea of what a fairy tale was. And she was going to get out
there. And fight like hell for hers.

move forward.
one day,
your heart
will be
as sure
as your footsteps.

You asked for a sign. You laughed defiantly at the universe and said—*if things are ever going to be alright again*, then show me. *Show me*. And then you got down on your knees and you prayed. And maybe up until then you didn't even know what you believed in. But you wanted someone—anyone—to tell you the one thing you've been longing to hear. That *it's going to be ok*. And you're going to be ok. And this is not where your story ends. Well, they did. Someone heard you. Because you're reading the words that are pouring out of my heart right now. Stream of consciousness. For you. Because someone, somewhere, wants you to know this. Wants you to see this. Wants you to understand that things aren't always going to be this hard and confusing and hurtful. That you are not forgotten. And your time *isn't up*. And you are going to get through this. And darling, sure, you've been through hell and back again. I know. You're down to your last piece of hope and faith. And your heart needs refilling. You're scared and tired and just want someone to take you by the hand and lead you through the darkness. Find your footing, sweet soul. And stay strong. Because your relief is coming. The clouds are lifting. The sun is peeking through. Your dawn is here.

yes.

you can.

and *that*
is where
your whole story
begins.

Your big heart. It's kind. And giving. And open. You give a lot of yourself, and so it seems people naturally flock to you—and have, all throughout your life—with their struggles. They know you'll *listen*. They know you'll *care*. And yes, they probably know you'll *help*, too. You're the person who takes on the weight of the world so it's just a little bit lighter for everyone else. You're the one who says *yes*. Who lends your money. And your time. And your car. And your patience. And that makes you *one of the good ones*. One of the people who change this world for the better. But I'm guessing, sometimes, that can make you pretty damn tired, too. And that's what you need to understand. We all do—the ones with the big hearts. Darling, you need to know where the line is. For you. Because there is a difference between being selfless and losing yourself. There is a difference between being giving and patient and sympathetic—and carrying the weight of the world for someone else. We all have a finite amount of strength. It's renewable, yes. But it can run out pretty quick when it's given away too freely. You have to keep some for you. And your own heart. And your own challenges. And most importantly, the hearts you love. So yes. Let people come to you. Let them set down the heavy load they are carrying. Let them share their story. But darling, when it's time for them to walk the roads of their life—remember this. No matter how much you love them or want to do it for them—that's not how it works. It's up to them—to each of us—to carry what's ours. And there is exactly one person who can change the weight of what we're each carrying. *Us.*

There had been times in her life when she could quite literally see the signs. The pieces—the messages—laid out perfectly for her to decipher. To understand. And that is when she would always know it was time. Finally. To let go, to *move on.* From a chapter—a part of her past—and step forward into a new life. Change was like that for her. Each and every time she felt she needed to change her life, the world seemed to push back—dragged its feet—with opportunities for her to do it. But when the world was ready—there it was. Every time. As clear and precise a message as if it were whispered directly in her ear. *Let go, sweet girl, and step forward.* It is time to see what comes next—time to train your eyes on the next beautiful horizon. You hear it calling—so follow it, darling, *follow it.* When you hear the world calling your name—when it's tugging you forward—you go. Those are the times you know you're in the middle of greatness. The pivotal, life-changing parts. And in the end, I guess you could say that girl learned to trust that call. As scary as it was to lean forward towards an unknown future—while stepping out of a comfortable past—she knew these were the times that meant the most. When her feet learned to trust that her heart led them well. Eyes forward, heart clear—she listens now. And without fear, steps out of her past—and walks forward. With faith. And hope. And an open heart, towards the world. The big, beautiful, new world that is calling her name.

it's ok,
    darling.
we all
pick a rose or two
  with one too many
      thorns.

She was one of those people who didn't believe in regrets. Not because she never wanted to go back and change something from the past—but because she believed in the *pieces*. She believed that *each and every piece of her life* was meant to fit where it fell—good, bad, and everything in between. But there was always one thing that challenged her life of no regrets. She had seen it in herself, and she had seen it in others. And it broke her heart every time. It made her want to believe in go-backs—in the ability to change how things had happened. Because for some reason, there is a phase in every girl's life—somewhere—where she stops valuing herself for a while. She selects the wrong heart—holds the wrong hand—and then lets it keep her caged. She allows it to steal her confidence and paint her into a corner and make her start to think she doesn't *sparkle* anymore. It's a dangerous heart, that one. And for this one phase of her life, it slowly strangles the joy out of her. Makes her feel trapped—as if she can't move forward and she can't go back. That heart makes her believe she isn't deserving of what she wants in this life. And that— that—is the part she wants to go back and redo. That whole thing. And *damn it* if every time she sees that look in the eyes of another soul, she doesn't wish everyone could rewind that phase. She wishes she could tell them how they don't have to go through it—they don't have to be broken and robbed of that joy that is supposed to infect their lives. And holding a hand—*holding a hand*—should never cage a soul. She wants to tell these girls—herself—that you deserve someone who shows up for you. Wants you. Believes in you. Thinks you hung the moon. And so now—since she's learned this—she just wants those other sweet hearts to know the truth. You are amazing. You are worth it. Don't ever let someone make you feel that you aren't. *Ever.*

you
are not
a reflection
of the hearts
that can't love you.
don't ever
use them
as your
mirror.

and maybe
it's impossible

to look through
eyes of reason
and eyes of love

at the
same time.

Love is blind. She knew it. She'd heard it her whole life. But she—like so many others—liked to think she was the exception. That she'd be able to see what everyone else could see. About her. And him. And them. That she'd be able to look through eyes of reason and eyes of love at the exact same time. And still know what she was looking at. And maybe eventually she could. But not before she learned this one the hard way. It's funny. Life. Often the *most important* lessons are the ones she wouldn't—couldn't—be spared from learning the hard way. Experience only. Sink or swim. *Battle scars.* And when it came to love, she knew now that this was how it went. She had to be a little blinded by a heart or two along the way. It was both a tragic and beautiful thing. But it would teach her. About her eyes, when paired with her heart. She'd learn how the heart could obscure things that were in plain sight to others. And yet lead her through the darkness just the same. She didn't know this all up front. Because she learned it's not easy to look through both eyes of reason and love at the same time. So she got a little walked on. But she learned. Oh, did she ever learn. And she carries her scars proudly now. Because they mean something. To her. To those who see them. They show that she knows what she wants. And what she doesn't. That she's been through a few battles. And won. They tell the world what she won't accept. But mostly, that she's ready. To see. To love. To feel. Because—yes, *because*—she's been hurt. She had to have the pain. So she could see the difference between the cost of playing the game—and the ones out to hurt her from the start. And never again— *never again*—would she mistake the two.

She was the kind of girl who changed hearts.

And eyes. She focused on making people *feel*. She didn't worry so much about what the world saw on the outside. Those were only the windows—and she wanted to know the fuel. She wanted to know what *moved* people—what drove them. She wanted to spend her time *making everybody* feel like somebody. To give the hearts she was with her undivided attention. And then she wanted to drink in the moments with them. The now. The beautiful string of pieces that assemble each of our lives. She chose to believe in people. To believe this old world was full of more good than bad—and her hopefulness made others believe, too. Her presence rejuvenated hearts. When they were weary—when the chaos and pace and uncertainty of the world plagued them—she somehow refreshed them. It was as if they were able to see the world through her eyes—if even for a short time. She wanted to do that for everyone. And she did. And when it came down to the ones her heart beat for—she was even more intentional. She knew not all hearts ended up together in the end. Even if they fit in some beautiful ways. So she loved with her whole self—went all in. But then listened. She listened to what her heart needed. And what it didn't. And because she listened, she knew when to let go. She wanted to be a good thief. She wanted to steal the negativity and chaos and hopelessness from the world. And maybe, people would say she stole hearts, too. But that's where it stopped. She could never steal from others what they could never get back. Time.

I'll tell you what happened. You told her to get out there and find her life. So she did.

You should have been careful what you told her. Because she *was listening*. When you challenged her to get out there and chase her dreams—she was planning. When you told her life would take her far—she was hoping. When you pushed her forward and asked her to find her life—she decided it was time. *So she did.* She traveled, without fear, away from her safe boundaries. From everything she'd known. She accepted the unknown and used uncertainty to pave a road to where she wanted to go. And along the way, she found love. And happiness. And kindness. She used the strength she earned fighting adversity and negativity as her walking stick. And life carried her. Carried her because she decided she'd use the winds, rather than fight them. And you know, she found that life she wanted—that she needed—because she was brave enough to try. She was honest enough to know she needed the universe to steer her part of the way. And sure, she lost things. But they weren't things she needed moving forward. And of course, sometimes, she wanted to look back. But in her heart, she knew that her eyes needed to stay pointed forward. That her heart needed to stay open. Because she was a believer. A dreamer. With starry eyes and a pure soul. She wanted big dreams and big love and purpose. And so that's exactly what she found.

Sometimes we have to get back to basics. Like, absolute, fundamental basics. The world is fast. And connected. And the more it shows us, the quicker it drains our batteries. The news. Oh—the news. Is there ever any good news anymore? Social media. Dating websites. Apps for anything and everything. We've become more connected than ever before, and yet so many of us feel totally disconnected. And so alone. We walk around, passing hundreds of people each day as we work off our to-do lists, fight traffic, wait in lines. We think of yesterday. And tomorrow. And next week. But not today. Not right now. We watch reality shows and talk in every detail about other people's lives. And yet we each long for a connection that's all our own. We live in a time when we can reach *every corner of the earth* by typing something into a browser, or opening an app. And yet what each of us wants is someone who knows every corner of us. Our hearts. Our past. Our future. And loves us like crazy for it. And that's where the math comes in. We all need to get focused at some point. And count all the things that matter. To us. To our lives. And then we need to subtract the negative. The news. The TV. The people. The jobs. The commute. To the largest degree that we can. And then we need to find what makes us happy. And we need to multiply it. Like crazy. We need to stop being *so connected* and look for *actual connections*. We need to draw our world close to us. And hang on like crazy to the things that matter. And go after like crazy the things we want. Start today, darling. I know it's not easy. But set your heart towards what's real. Because that is where happiness is waiting for you.

just
let her
be her.
the universe
will take care
of the rest.

want
the key
to happiness?
just be
what you are.

Cheer for people.
There's enough happy for us all. Promise.

She knew the truth. There would always be someone with *more*. More opportunities. More friends. More money. More car. More house. And there would always be someone with *better*. A better body. A better school. A better job. More and better were everywhere. Sure. And she could see those things as competition. And compare. But she doesn't. The amazing features and lives and opportunities of others don't make her unhappy. Or jealous. They don't make her think she needs to be someone else or have something else. She would never want to dim someone else's light because it was shining in her eyes. She knows those uniquely beautiful things she recognizes in others are what make them amazing. That's *their* light. *Their* sparkle. And that's ok, because she has some of those things too. We all do. And the key is to see the beauty—not the competition. Because there is enough sunshine for us all. I so totally promise you that. So cheer for people. Build them up. And let them shine. Darling, please—*just let them shine*.

it's funny.
all the things
i couldn't control
are what
made me
who i am.

I know that sometimes those worries can take over. They can talk over that positive voice within you. They can steamroll the *don't worry, there's a reason for all this*. They can replicate and grow—and sometimes, no matter how hard you try—*they just win*. They win, even though the rational part of you knows worry doesn't help, and even though you know way more than half of what you worry about works out just fine in the end. Well, when that happens—sometimes you just need some outside reassurance. Maybe even from someone you've never met, a world away, writing to you in a book you never knew you always needed to read. So let me tell you, darling, what you need to hear. *It will be ok.* It will. The world works through unfinished chapters and ties up loose ends. The universe will bring the people together that are destined to be together. And yes, *time will teach you why*. Always. Not on your timeline—but on the perfect timeline for you. Because, darling? Those two timelines *are* different. So let me just tell you tonight to hang on. Let me just tell you to—if you can—set down all those heavy thoughts. Those questions. Those worries. And let tomorrow come to you. Peacefully. Because even now, when you're way too close to it to see the big picture, things are working. Working to come together. And the universe is getting ready to show you the beautiful reason it made you wait.

you're worried
you missed

your chance.

but right now,
the universe
is unfolding
the **beautiful** reason

it made you wait.

All around you, storms will rage. Things will be uprooted and tossed around. Chaos and uncertainty will infiltrate calm, and yet—you will be unaffected. Untouched by the damaging winds and rains of this life. Darling, it's about *strategy*. And perspective. Think of the eye of the hurricane. It is calm—a strange oasis amidst the worst of life's chaos. All around it, the fiercest winds and rains the universe can muster are made. Swirled and strengthened—around and around and around. But within—it's precisely the opposite. Sunshine instead of clouds. Calm in place of winds. *Peace*. The eye of the storm never knows the rest of it. It's just a little spot of refuge. The crack in the wall of darkness that brings light from the heavens to the ravaged earth. And maybe that's what life is about, sweet soul. Finding the eye of our hurricanes and spending our lives dancing within it. Moving as it does. Trying our best to avoid the strongest winds. And using the ones we can't avoid to push us in the direction we never knew we always needed to go.

i **promise**
you this:

your eyes
don't know
everything.

You're going to break your own heart, sweet soul, if you keep loving that person you think one day they'll be. Chances are, you've already learned this one this hard way. It's who you are. When you love someone—you love all of them, don't you? Who they were, who they are—and yes, you love that best version of themselves you know *they could one day be*. And that's the part that gets you, sweet girl. That *potential* part. And here's the hard lesson: you *cannot love that person*. You can't. Oh, I know you *have*. And you may one day try again. But that has heartbreak written all over it. And here's why: *that is not who they are*. That might not even be who they want to be. So you have to stop falling in love with that ghost. That shadow. It's not real, sweet girl. It's just not. Love who they were. Love their scars and bruises and past and insecurities. Love them for who they are. With their faults and quirks and beautiful dreams about what they want in life. And stop there. Encourage them like crazy to chase after what they want. Be proud of them. Give them the fuel and hope and encouragement to be who they want to be. But don't love that person yet, darling. Because one too many hearts has been shattered by falling in love with someone that may never be. You have to love people where they are—not where you think they're going. So do yourself a favor. And learn this one well. Your hand can't be holding who they are—while your heart falls in love with who they may be. It's not fair to them. And it's not fair to you. So protect your heart, darling. Let your eyes see what's real. And then let your heart fall in love with that same thing.

sometimes
the spark
existing between
two hearts will smolder.
but the fire
within your
own heart
should be untouchable,
sweet soul.

untouchable.

She always thought it was ironic. How her eyes showed her exactly what she was focused on in life. When she wanted so much to have someone to love—all around her, the world had someone to love. When she wanted to be fitter—to lose weight—everyone around her was already thin and beautiful. It was as if the world only showed her what her heart wanted most. And every single time she saw it living in others, it *hurt*. It hurt, that was, until she finally learned what was happening. When her heart wanted something—someone to love, to start a family, to save more money, to lose weight—her eyes were going to show her just that. And depending on how much she wanted it—maybe *only* that. And the truth was, the whole world didn't have everything she wanted. That was just part of the lesson. And she knew it. And so she started teaching her heart to be patient. And training her eyes *to see* more. She knew these things took time. And no matter how much her heart wanted something, she wasn't going to speed up the timing the universe already had planned. She didn't have to run the race—competing against every other person to be first. It wasn't her against everyone else. It was just her. And that's when peace flooded in. When it stopped being some big competition—she stopped worrying about being left behind. She stopped worrying whether things would or wouldn't happen. Or when. Or how. She knew her life was packed with surprises and good things and life would unfold her purpose. In time. And that's when she decided to stop measuring her life with someone else's measuring stick. This was about *her*. And she knew her heart would lead her.

The only difference was, now she knew who was worth the risk.

Her heart had loved and been loved. It had questioned and been certain. It had gone through a little hell—broken and been pieced back together. She has a few people on a list somewhere that hurt a little too much to think much about. And there are a whole bunch of others that have faded gently into her past. They don't hurt. There are no loose ends. They were just building blocks. And yes, there had been a time or two when she had wanted to give up the trusting and the hoping. Times when she doubted she'd ever put a vulnerable, open heart in someone else's hands. Times she thought she knew every part of a soul—only to find out she couldn't know those parts *of their* heart. The parts that make them be the *no*. The *not right now*. The wrong one for her. But I guess she doesn't have a heart like that. The hardened kind. As much as she'd like it to—that heart of hers just won't switch off. It just loves—fully, completely—totally. So she isn't going to hold back. She's going to let that heart love and know it might break. Because that's the gamble, and she wants to play. She isn't going to change the intensity of her love. But you *can be damn sure* she's going to change the quality of the people who get it. She's willing to risk it. Truth is, it's just that now she knows who is worth the risk. And that, she has found, may very well be the lesson of her lifetime.

But darling, sometimes the bravest thing you can do is never look back.

The world tells her a lot of things. To never leave things unfinished. To never walk away mad. It barrages her with advice. Constantly. It tells her *everyone* has a purpose for her life. But what it doesn't say quite so loudly—with quite as much certainty—is that she doesn't have to wait around to find out what that purpose is. Because it will find her, when it's ready. What the world *needs* to tell her is that she doesn't have to stay in a situation that's hurting her heart. And even that it's ok to love someone who *isn't right* for her life. It needs to remind her that one of the most important things she can do is learn how to say no. That this is not right for me. And mean it. She is the kind of girl who hates hurting others. Sometimes at the cost of breaking her own heart. But she's also strong. Extremely strong. And so she's going to learn this lesson, hard as it may be. Sometimes the heart and the brain get a little disconnected from the feet. But eventually they all end up in the same place. And so she knows now—really knows—what it takes to let her heart lead her. It means sometimes letting her feet lead her forward while her brain is holding her back. It means accepting an end so she can chase a new beginning. It means being confident in her footsteps. Because she knows that sometimes *the right thing* isn't to work through the *minute* details. It isn't to stay until you've tried every single option. It isn't talking and talking and trying. At some point, it gets down to the most basic question of them all. Does it work? And there are times that the answer is quite simply—and quite precisely—just *no*. So that girl has learned to let herself be ok with endings. Because she knows that there will be times in her life where the *trying* needs to stop. And the absolute bravest thing she can do is *walk away*. Knowing that it's not called giving up. It's called being strong. And intentional. And knowing what is best for *her* and her heart. And so that is what she does when it gets to that point. She finds the strength within her to *begin* again.

Maybe part of her, back then, wondered why a little too much. *Why* something didn't happen. Or did. Why things happened slower or faster than she wanted them to—than they did for everyone else. Why she made the mistakes she did. Or didn't find the answers she wanted. And why—*why*—was a slippery slope. Because asked too many times in a row, she knew it had a much larger effect on her life than she intended. It made her powerless. It put all the power of action into the hands of some ambiguous and ill-defined force. The unknown. And that was something she couldn't control. And wasn't her. And that wasn't ok—because she *wasn't* a victim. She wasn't a product of circumstance. She wasn't going to be left behind or forgotten. She was perfectly designed. And she was here on this earth for a very distinct, and very specific purpose. And yes, she was damn well going to find it. She knew the universe wasn't spending its time blessing her or punishing her. It was just responding to the energy she put out into it. And that's the exact moment she asked the last *why me.* She knew the truth. Things were going to happen or they weren't. They were going to change or stay the same. But either way, she was going to be in control *of her.* She wasn't just planning to survive this life—putting up with what came her way. She was planning to live it like crazy. She was a warrior. A fighter. The damn driver of her own life. She stood tall and looked the universe and the future and the unknown and the chaos and the uncertainty straight in the eye. And she whispered. *Try me.*

i am done
surviving.
it is time
to live.

but darling,
that is not

fire.

it's *dawn.*

It is not easy. Life. It's a roller coaster at best, isn't it? A beautifully chaotic seesaw of loving and losing, learning and growing, dreaming and planning. And for every hard-earned victory—for every single thing we can *celebrate*—there are a million drafts that came before it. Complete with the bruises and tears and battle scars. Yes, life is tough. It takes things from us. And beats us up. And twists and turns us around on paths we thought were going to be straight. We lose the people we thought would be our forever and we make mistakes we think we can never fix. We face challenges we could never dream of and feel beauty we could never see. And we learn how many times a heart can be placed in the hopeful hands of someone else—but then also stitched carefully back together by our hands alone. And that's ok. It all is. Because yes, life is tough. No one will ever tell you it isn't. But you know what? *You* are tough, too. You are. You've survived every single one of your toughest days yet—and you're still out there fighting and working and growing. And maybe you feel a little sad—or weak—sometimes, but that's ok. You aren't giving up. You're stronger than that. And every single day you pick yourself up and you begin again. With hope. With love. With faith. Knowing that today could be the day everything changes. And you can survive whatever comes your way, sweet soul, by knowing the trick. Keep a little fire. And then make sure no matter what, that the fire that burns within you *always burns stronger* than the fire that rages around you.

She was too much for him. She gave too much.

Understood too much. Loved too much. She was infinitely patient and understanding of his restless heart. Of his broken soul. When she came upon the pieces, she wanted so badly to put him back together. She saw in them the man he *used* to be. *Wanted* to be. *Almost* was. So she waited. And waited. And waited. Maybe too long. For him to be ready. To love her like she loved him. To heal. To see the potential of the man he could be. She saw him with clear eyes. And a pure, innocent heart. She loved him. With a depth she couldn't quantify—and he could never understand. But he couldn't get there. He couldn't see himself through the same eyes. His heart was too broken and his wounds were too deep. And she saw it eventually. Her heart broke a little for him. For them. But she got it. And while her heart longed *to fix him*, the universe whispered no. *Not this time*. Not this heart. And maybe in time he would learn to see himself in a fraction of the light she saw him in. And although she'd hope for that—she could no longer wait. Her love wasn't enough for the both of them. And she deserved to be loved. For who she was. And what she was. By a heart that was ready. And came willing. She was a beautiful soul. That wanted so much to change his heart. Make him see the potential and depth of what they could have. But to carry true love, it takes more than just one pair of hands. And she wasn't the kind of girl who could change her heart. Just so he could learn to carry it.

and maybe
what you
taught me

was simply
how to
say good-bye.

Sometimes she goes back. To that place. That beautiful yet *somewhat dangerous* place she never lets herself linger very long. Because like quicksand, it tries to pull her back. And she *won't* walk backwards. Sometimes she lets herself go back to the good times, though. She lets herself think of the sparkle she had in her eyes. The butterflies in her stomach. She lets herself go back to the place that love grew so readily. So freely. She wanted to be everything back then—everything as long as it meant loving *that* one heart. It was a roller coaster. A twisted crazy chaos-filled wonderland. And god, how she loved him. Like she never knew she could love another heart. So when it broke, it tore her apart and whispered calmly to her at the same time. *He* was wrong. And *this* was right. The answer was no, even with all that love there. As it turns out, she found, love isn't the only ingredient. And she couldn't love enough for the both of them. Letting go of love like that—it's next to impossible. The part that knew she deserved someone who met her halfway—that girl keeps her feet moving forward. But the girl who loved him? That girl looks back every now and then on those times. On *that* kind of love. And *she doesn't* wish for him. No. But she does hope and pray she finds what grew in her then. To know that kind of love is out there. That is what propels her forward, even if it asks her to look back. There was a lesson—there always was. His was to awaken her heart and fill it with the kind of love she deserved. But when she learned he wasn't the one who could keep it filled, he taught her the second most important lesson of her lifetime. How to say good-bye.

Don't ever let them tell you it wasn't love.

Don't. The heart is *complex* with all its wantings. With what it chases and wants to have chase it back. How and why it latches on to other hearts—even when it makes little sense to anyone else. That's just a portion of its beauty. It's one of those things that can't be coerced. It can't be forced. It just *is*. And it grows within us, for a lifetime, changing everything. But darling, it's *yours* to define. It's yours to *feel*. It's often—often—going to make no sense to anyone else. They may question. They may push. They may say they know you better than you know yourself. Well, *maybe* in some ways they do. But not in this one. Love is yours. Don't ever let them tell you you're *too young* or you *can't possibly* understand. Don't let them question how you could possibly love someone like that. Sure—we all eat a few lies when our hearts are hungry. And we all stumble upon a few roses with too many thorns. But that's how we learn. And that's not an experience we should ever be shielded from. So *yes*. You're going to love some people you probably shouldn't. And it's going to make no sense to anyone else. And that's ok. The heart has reasons which reason can never understand. Be strong, sweet girl. Question everything in your life if you need to. Ask why you waited so long and why you couldn't see and maybe, why it is the two of you just couldn't get it right. But never, never let them tell you it wasn't love.

time
will teach
you why.

Some days, she woke up with that slight pit in her stomach—the tenderness in her shoulders. The worry—over tomorrow and yesterday and right and wrong creeping in. And that worry would sit there—forming the lens by which she would see everything that *is* and *was* and *might be*. It hurt her. Slowly, a little bit each day. She used to wonder if this was all there was. And whether there was really a plan for her. She used to think she'd had her chance. But she doesn't anymore. Her life is a series of chapters. And they end and begin. Some are longer than others. Some end abruptly with fewer answers than she'd hoped. But they're *chapters* all the same. And no single chapter gets to decide how everything is going to end. And that's when she stopped letting that worry seep into her. It's when she learned to *let go* a little—and stopped looking back so much. It's when she gave up thinking about things that hadn't happened yet. For her. And she let go of longing for answers and yesterday and the main characters of the chapters she'd already written. And you know, she got a little excited. About moving forward. And meeting all the amazing people and having all the amazing experiences she knew in every part of her heart were coming next. And then she smiled. *Today*. What a beautiful word.

I'll tell you why she made it. It had nothing to do with an easy road. It wasn't because she got a few lucky breaks and some good opportunities. It wasn't because the universe favored her—rolled out a red carpet and gave her a map for her life. No. That girl made it because she *never* quit. Never. She knew exactly what she wanted. And she kept those eyes and that heart focused on just that. She never made a place in her life for the haters and nonbelievers. She refused to accept that what she wanted wasn't within her reach. That girl took a million punches and kept rolling. She walked a million miles and kept walking. She made it because her heart never got tired. It housed a passion and a drive that nothing in the world could take. Or diminish. And the world tried—*oh, did it ever try*. But the fire within her was untouchable. It was that simple. And that beautiful.

in
a world
where
she can
be anything

she is
kind.

Someone once told her that taking her life seriously was imperative. But taking herself seriously was disastrous. She stored that tidbit away. She liked how it sounded—but it never quite made sense to her. How she could take her life seriously—and be driven and focused—without taking herself too seriously. It wasn't something she understood yet. But she would. Somewhere down the road, after life had shown her a few hands, she would get it. Life *was* serious. It was full of challenge and progress. Losing and winning. Heart-wrenching loss. And earth-shattering love. It was full of moments that changed everything. And years that changed nothing. But life was her series of battles. In her war. And she was the only one who could fight it. From the first day, to the last day. This was her burden. And yet, her canvas, too. So yes, life was full of serious things. She saw that every day. But what she learned was she didn't have to take herself so seriously in the process. So amidst the chaos and the uncertainty and the never-ending battles— that girl learned to laugh. At herself—when she made mistakes. At the situation—when it spun out of control. At the irony. And the beauty. And the craziness of all the pieces. She learned to find the humor in the situation. And when she couldn't see it right away, she slowed down to look for it. Because she knew, finally, what the truth was. There was nothing in life so hard that it couldn't be made easier by the way she approached it. And that, she knew, was a truly powerful thing.

We often spend too long analyzing. Assessing.

Weighing all the perspectives and angles carefully. We second-guess what someone or something meant. We *justify*. And make *excuses*. We give second, and third, and fifteenth chances. For some reason, we tend to take a long time to accept an answer we already know is right. And that's not a bad thing—that we want to *believe* in others. To see the best in them. But when it comes down to your life—to *all of our lives*—we have to know one thing really well. Our hearts. We have to know what we will and won't accept. We have to learn to listen to that little twinge, that little hesitation, that little part of us that tells us when something isn't right. And then we need to learn the second hardest thing. *Trusting* it. Trusting those feelings enough to make our feet carry us away from those people or things. Because the truth is, you already have what you need to find that amazing life you've always wanted. To find the person you've always wanted. You just have to use that heart of yours to steer you. Towards what it knows is right. And away—away—from what it knows is not. And you don't need a reason. If it's not right for your life, darling, then it's not right for your life. Muster the courage, and learn early how to walk away from anything that you know isn't meant for your heart. It's hard. But it's worth it. Because in the end, it gives you what you need most. Space for what is.

Maybe the word miracle is just misunderstood.

Because when most of us witness a miracle or pray for a miracle, we're hoping for it to *work*. Praying for it to *work out*. A miracle is when we get what we ask for—what we've dreamed of—what we've hoped for. Right? Sure. But you know, it's more than that, I think. Maybe the miracle isn't always the yes. Maybe sometimes it's the no. Or the *wait-for-it*. Or *the trust-me*. Or the *not-right-now*. Maybe the timing really is everything and as much hoping and praying and negotiating as we may do with the universe—it just doesn't give in. Because *it knows* what we don't. What we *can't*. It knows that our life—the right one for us—just comes along when it's ready. And while we're wishing something would happen sooner, things are actually coming together. And when we're crying over the heart that got away, someone else is falling in love with us—in that moment—just as we are. And I don't know why the *hard no* comes for any of us. The people that are taken too soon. The ones we love with the very breath we breathe. But I still believe—and know—that as hard as those chapters are, sweet soul, there *is* a reason. It's yours to discover. To explore. Just don't ever give up—no matter how hard it gets. Trust it. Because there are so many miracles in your life—and maybe the *no* and the *later* and the *not-right-now* aren't the universe punishing you or leaving you behind. Maybe those are the real miracles. We just don't see them until the whole picture comes together. Because when we do—and we will—we understand why it couldn't have worked out any other way. So don't leave before the miracle happens. And P.S. Maybe it already *has*.

her heart
knew the truth.
one day,
she would be
someone's greatest
adventure.

she could wait.

She doesn't want just any old heart. And she isn't looking for someone she can just *live* with. Or spend time with. She could have that. Sure. But to her, love came painted with a full picture. It was a word, defined by an entire lifetime of watching. And noticing. The gentle hand. The sparkling eye. The us-against-the-world. The *til-the-last-breath*. And so that's what she wants. The kind of love she can't live *without*. The kind that changes everything. *Is* everything. She knows she can find a million people who she'd have fun with. Who could share stories and moments and smiles. But she wants so much more than that. She wants the spark. The excitement. The mystery. The depth. She wants the kind of love that makes the world *stop* and *start* spinning all at once. She wants a heart who *connects* with hers. Who doesn't want her to be anyone else *but her* and can't imagine *not* being beside her. She wants the one who won't agree with everything she says—but will still defend her. And stand beside her. And stand up for her. Someone who complements her. And *compliments* her. But means it. The true *other* half. Someone who brings opinions and perspectives and input. And opens her eyes to things she hasn't seen. She wants it all. The one who meets her and finally understands what it's all about. *Because* of her. And *them*. Together. And so in a world always pushing and asking and planning—she holds up her hand. And smiles. Because she knows what she's looking for. And she'll wait.

It's funny how it works, isn't it? One hundred people can tell you good things—compliment you, build you up, support you—and then *one* person can crack the armor. With their negativity. Or their *mean* heart. Or their *hurtful* soul. One person can size you up—see the one and only place you're vulnerable—and take out their arrow. It's crazy. We don't even *like* these people—hell, we often don't even *know* them—but for some reason we let them affect how we feel about ourselves. And our potential. And our beauty. And our talent. And our ability to go after what we want. That one perfectly selected insult rattles around in our heads for weeks. Or years. And it stays a vulnerability. For us. For a really, *really* long time. All because one person—*one* person—didn't think some part of us was right. Was good enough. But that's *their* opinion. And to be honest, they're certainly entitled to it. But that doesn't mean you have to take those things into your heart, into your *image* of you. You can choose to be built up by those who love you. And strengthened by those who believe in you. And darling, you can develop a confidence that is unaffected by those perfectly placed insults—hurtful words—and negativity. Turn your face away from anyone who sends those kinds of words out into the universe. And know this. They aren't really trying to hurt you. Most of the people who need to break others down are doing it because inside, they are just a little broken themselves. And they're trying to protect themselves with a little offense. But you? You need to spend your time focusing on the ones who love you. Not the ones who don't. We have barely a hundred years on this earth—if we're lucky—and there just isn't enough time to worry about the ones who *hurt* your heart. Your focus is the ones who *are* your heart.

and maybe
the great
secret
is light.

not
the kind
you search for.

the kind
you carry.

It scares most people. When the darkness starts to roll in. But not her. She stands bravely at the precipice—and looks defiantly into the night. Daring it to bring its worst. Its darkest, deepest, most impenetrable darkness. Because she *can take it.* And last *throughout* it. She is unafraid. Unafraid because she knows that darkness is not the opposite of light. It's just the *other side* of light. This darkness—that instills fear into the hearts of the world—doesn't threaten her. She faces it. Head-on. Because she knows it's only a matter of time. Before its reign is over. And she can wait.

Oh, believe me, you didn't break her. You couldn't break her if you tried. And I'm sure you did try, didn't you? But I've got news for you, darling. Life can't break that soul of hers. That heart of hers. She has survived tornadoes. And hurricanes. Ripping things from her grasp while she tried like hell to hold on. And it wasn't *just* you. Life tried to do it, too. Threw her storm after storm. But she just stood there—leaning into the wind. Unwavering. Undeterred. Unbroken. Knowing eventually even storms get tired. But not her. Like a rock, she just waited it out. Knowing nothing lasts forever. *Nothing.* And when the winds died down, she emerged. Stronger. And when she walked forward, into her new life, she was happy. Because she knew now—she really knew—that she was stronger than whatever life could throw at her. She'd done it before. And she could do it again. She wouldn't be broken. She just wasn't *that kind* of girl.

They tell her she needs to have a *plan*. That she needs to know what she's *going after*. What she's *working for*. Who she *is*. Who she *wants* to be. They tell her she needs to know *where* she wants to go to school. And *what* she wants to study when she gets there. That she needs to know where she *wants to live*. What she wants to *do*. The world shouts at her. And calls to her. Tells her there is no time. And she has to know. Now. That she has to choose. But *not* her. She knows better. She knows she doesn't need to have all the answers. She doesn't even need to know all the questions. Because she will decide who she wants to be a million times in her life. And maybe they will all be the same. Or maybe, each and every time she chooses, she'll be something brand new. She will be shaped every day of her life. By everything around her. And one day, all the drafts will add up to something amazing. *Her*. That best version of herself she's working so hard to be. And she'll get to that place. She will. Just let her be *her*. The universe will take care of the rest.

she never wanted
to blend in.
she wanted
to be
fluorescent pink
in a world
of gray.

Do yourself a favor, and learn how to walk away. I

know. It goes contrary to everything you believe—*everything* you've been told. You are patient. And kind. And you tend to give people more chances than they deserve. Even when they don't appreciate it. Even when there's no chance they'd reciprocate that kindness and patience. And so at some point, you are going to have to teach yourself a hard lesson. How and *when* to walk away. It's not giving up. Or being unkind. It's not unfair or mean. It's you taking control. Refusing to be taken advantage of. Telling them loud and clear that you aren't someone people can walk all over. And most of all, that your *kindness* should never be mistaken for weakness. It's hard, I know. But you are going to have to learn what it looks like. That line. Where it stops being about helping them and waiting for them and being patient with them. And it becomes about you. And seeing the truth. At some point, darling, they've proven that they *aren't* going to change. They aren't going to want what you want. They aren't going to do what they keep saying they'll do. And you need to teach yourself to walk away. Your excuses need to stop. Your patience needs to run out. Your bending over backwards needs to cease. Because it's not a limitless source. And if you constantly give it all to the ones who don't appreciate it, you're going to run out. For the ones who will. So yes, sometimes the greatest thing you can do for your life, for your heart, for your happiness—is to walk away. Away from what's holding you back. Away from what's hurting you. Making you doubt. And yes, learn how to respect *yourself* enough to see when they aren't respecting *you* enough. It's scary and unknown, what comes next. I know. But the truth is, what comes next is going to be *so* much better. Because you are a different person now. Teach them, darling. Teach them how to treat you by what you accept. And most importantly, by what you won't.

Your heart. That sweet, delicate, trusting heart.
It loved the wrong person. It gave all the right pieces—it just chose the wrong one to give them to. You have spent *so much time* analyzing what went wrong—what you could have done differently. How you gave so much. And they returned so little. You've been *over and over* the end. The beginning. The moments. The milestones. And it just won't make sense. But then it does. And the lesson, darling—quite simply—is that *it was a lesson*. A chapter. And what you take away from this experience is going to be unique. But life-changing. Your heart just learned the hardest lesson it will ever have to learn. How to have the capacity to love enough for the both of you. And it's tired. Because it shouldn't *have to* love enough for two. And honestly, it can't. That's not how it's designed. So give yourself a break. Stop analyzing. Stop looking back. And move forward. That sweet, happy heart of yours is going to get what it needs. And deserves. And your time is coming. It is. And just think—if you loved the wrong one that much—think of how amazing it's going to be to love the right one.

that was
your chapter.
but **this**
is *my* story.

She heard them. Each and every time they told her she couldn't do it. She wouldn't get there. She didn't have what it takes. She wasn't smart enough. Or strong enough. Or witty enough. She didn't have the right look. Or personality. Or approach. She didn't *think* the right way. She had heard them, sure. But she hadn't *listened*. She hadn't taken those words and made them part of her. She hadn't used them to beat herself down. Or question whether she was good enough. What she did do, however, is store them away. She stored them away as strength. Motivation. Inspiration. Part of what fueled her journey. It wasn't their fault. They couldn't see it yet. They didn't understand what drove her. What type of perseverance lived in that heart. But they would. Because she would do what she wanted to do. And go where she wanted to go. And be who she wanted to be. And all those nonbelievers did one very important thing for her. They pushed her forward. Forward—into that life and person she knew she'd one day be. They pushed her enough to realize she wasn't made to be a passenger. So eyes forward and heart clear—she slipped confidently behind the wheel. And she never looked back.

i guess
you could
say

it felt like
waking up

or being
born.

because
finally,
there she was.

her.

I will tell you as many times as you need to hear

it. You are enough. You are so totally, incredibly enough. Yes, I know we are all on a journey to be better. To *fix* ourselves. To be a little fitter, healthier, happier, financially secure, patient, loving, more present. Whatever it is, we are all out there trying to make each and every day better than the day before. We are. So know this. Darling, even if you don't get there—to that place you want so much to be—I'll say it again. You are *enough*. Right now. With your past. With your mistakes. With the weight you want to lose. With the things you wish you had done. Hadn't done. Should have done. You are enough, just as you are. That perfectly imperfect version of you today. And here's why. The hardest part of living is realizing you can be both a masterpiece and a work in progress at the same time. But you can. You are. So don't lose hope. Don't get down on yourself. Don't keep comparing yourself to what you see around you. What and who your friends are—what social media and TV and magazines tell you that you have to be. Darling, go to that place within you. The place that defines who you really are and what you really want. And let that part drive your life. You are enough. Just as you are. Today. Right now. Even as you are working so hard to become someone else. You are enough. And that's a beautiful thing.

It has stuck with her. That line. She couldn't pinpoint where or when she'd heard it—but nevertheless, it had stuck. Those words—*your prayers are always answered, just not on the exact timeline you may wish for.* How true they were—and how *well* they had guided her heart. Wisdom was ever changing, she figured. At each and every point in her life, she thought she'd been innately in tune with the world and the way it worked. She'd always thought—for as much chaos as the universe threw her way—that she was *pretty damn good* at rolling with the punches. At figuring out where to place her next step. But it never failed—never—to amaze her how little she actually knew about what the world had in store for her. Every day. Every year. Every decade. Things were ever changing her. Surprising her. Amazing her. The things she wished for last year—they were *so* different now. The things she had worried about last week—they had worked out just fine. The people she thought would be her forevers ended up being her almosts—and life—life had pieced together a canvas for her that she was starting to really love. No, she didn't have everything she wanted. And hell, she had it *far* from figured out. But her eyes and her heart had grown through the years—and they were starting to know what to ask for. Her prayers and her dreams and her wishes—they became a lot less specific. They weren't for things or people. No. Now, they were for happiness and love and a peaceful heart. She knew she didn't know exactly what she would need down the road. So she was just going to pray that the universe would arm her as it saw fit. Taking away the things she wouldn't need—and giving her the things she would. Things were falling into place. She could see it—she could *feel* it. But until they did, she was going to keep believing. Keep praying. Keep hoping. And let time take care of the rest.

the world
is full
of possible.

She was here. In this moment. In whatever it was. However it felt. Happy or stressful. Frustrated or at peace. Wishing or content. *Here.* And some part of her knew that time—these moments—were the ones that slipped away into years. The everyday ones. The ones where she was hoping or dreaming or wishing for tomorrow. Or next week. Or some other faraway horizon. These moments were the ones she wanted to use. She wanted to stop letting them *so easily* slip away from her. Letting whole days go by where *things were ok* or *fine* or *it's almost Friday.* She wanted to change. She wanted to be more present. To drink in the random Tuesdays. The nights she was working too late. The days when everything went wrong. The traffic mornings. The days full of only errands. And to-do lists. Because the truth was, when she added it all up, she knew those moments and days were going to tip the scale. There would be more *everyday days* than Fridays and birthdays and holidays and milestones. So she was going to find a way to use them. And smile through them. And be happy and thankful. And grateful. For being able to do all those plain, simple, everyday things. Because in her heart she knew that even those days, one day, would be sweet memories. Of independence. And simplicity. And focus. So on a random, regular old everyday day, she decided to change her life. Things were far from perfect. She had a ton to do and so many things to worry about. But she was going to live this day like she was never going to get it back. Because she knew the truth. She wouldn't.

She had found her voice. Finally. Gone were the days she would let them think she didn't have an opinion. A side. Something important to say. No more would her kindness be mistaken for weakness—her quiet demeanor for indifference. That was yesterday. This was today. And although *that* girl was learning who she was and what she wanted—*this* girl did have something to say. And she was going to damn well say it. She knew it wasn't volume that demanded attention in this world—but rather—intelligence, intuition, and confidence. She knew who she was now. And although she knew it wouldn't please everyone—she also knew she wouldn't be swayed by them either. Her voice was just the product of a strong and confident heart. One that grew from experience. And loss. And joy. And heartache. And mistakes. And you know, there was something truly beautiful about that voice of hers. Because no matter what came out of her mouth—others respected it. They respected it, because she'd learned that her voice was heard more when her ears listened first. And so it was. A girl who didn't know what she wanted became one that did. One who knew how to ask for—and accept nothing less than—what she wanted. A quiet, beautiful confidence. That demanded the attention of her little corner of the world. That invited her onto the stage of her own life. And let her become—finally—exactly the girl she never knew she was always meant to be.

*just promise
you will
never
be afraid
to be afraid.*

The longer she lives, the clearer it becomes. Beauty has a source. A well. And it bubbles out into something that can be seen with the eyes. When people see it—they are drawn to it. When they're asked—they *can't quite* describe it. Some call it magic. Some have no words for it at all. But beauty—*real beauty*—changes eyes. And opens hearts. She has seen it. But it's rare. She watches as the good bodies and the stylish clothes pass her by. So many people who would look amazing on the cover of a magazine. But that's not who she wants to look up to. To be like. To love. So she waits. To be inspired by the *fire* of a soul.

Today, I'm going to need you to smile. No matter how you feel. At least once—but preferably for most of the day. Show your teeth. *Even* if you hate smiling with your teeth. I need you to get out there today and start throwing around some happy. Smile because you're grateful. For the little things. For the things you don't even think about having. *But do.* Get out there and touch the world. Maybe even change it. You probably don't have everything you want. But if you're honest, you probably do have most of what you need. So, take this moment—this day—and put all the things you're worried about aside. Yes, I know you're busy. And there is so much to do. Don't let yourself get caught up in the stress and the chaos. Remember what it's all about. Put your to-do list away for today. Call up the friends who make your face hurt from laughing so hard. And make that your priority. Watch a movie that is full of hope and a happy ending. Eat something you haven't had in a million years. And just smile. Smile because you know this old world is never going to be perfect. And that's alright—because you don't focus on what you can't change. You know where your corner is. And your smile today will change you first. And after it changes you, something else starts to happen. Ripples. So get out there and shake things up.

ok,
but if life
won't
give it to her,

then she is
just going to

get out there

and create
the world
she wants
to be a part of.

Every now and then, a heart comes along like hers.
Deep. Pure. And true. One not riddled with hate and bitterness. One that somehow still infuses a limitless supply of *hope* and *potential* and *light* into the world. Up until you meet a heart like hers—you'll think you control it all. Can control it all. You'll have one-year plans and five-year plans. You'll have goals by 25 and 30 and 40. You'll think you have it all figured out. That you are the artist of your whole life. Well, maybe. But just partly. Because these hearts change you like nothing you've ever experienced. Maybe you call them a sister. Or a brother. Or a friend. If you're really lucky—you'll call them yours. Yours. They infuse your whole life with purpose and light. They make you look at the same things differently. They change you. *Completely.* Totally. Fully. And maybe they just dance into your life for a season. Or perhaps you'll be lucky enough to know one for a lifetime. But one thing is true. After them, you *get it.* Sometimes the universe has better plans for you than you have for yourself. And sometimes, someone else gets to hold the paintbrush. And paint a little part of your masterpiece.

Truth be told, she found strength because she had to. In life, that's how she'd always found it. Things happened, and she knew it was her decision. Let it beat her. Or decide she'd be stronger than whatever tried to break her. So yes, she was *used* to strength. And finding it in her weakest, most vulnerable moments. But this time, it was different. This time she was holding on like hell to the thing that was tearing at her grasp. And when she couldn't hold on anymore—when it just danced off without her—she knew what she had to do. Find the strength to keep going. To understand. To believe. And that she did. But what she wasn't expecting—hidden between the holding on and letting go—was what came next. She had never wanted to let go. But it was time. So the universe forced her hand. And after the tears dried—and her heart was pieced back together, her eyes cleared. And it was there. That thing she never knew she'd been missing. Happiness.

Life was a beautiful thing. After she'd seen a few sunrises and sunsets, she was finally starting to see how it all fit together. It wasn't random chaos. It wasn't accidental. It wasn't unplanned. She *got* that now. Every single heart that crossed her path was actually meant to be there—meant to change her. Sometimes a little at a time— and others, all at once. She finally understood that she wasn't going to be able to predict who and what changed her. And she wasn't going to be able to perfectly plan her future just because she wanted to. No, life always had better plans for her than she did for herself. It was just slower—more deliberate—in unfolding its grand design. So she learned to be patient. And the longer she lived, the more she loved that mystery. Those parts of her that changed—grew—blossomed— because of some heart that crossed her path. Walked with her. For a mile or a thousand miles. She had learned so much about herself that way. It was crazy how someone could force her to be someone she never knew she always was. How they could make her discover who she really was and what she really wanted. How they could divert her away from some things and towards others. A well-placed comment— or a massive heartbreak—it made no difference. Every single one of them was a lesson. And she really grew to love those experiences. It was crazy. But she did. She had grown tired of worrying and planning and controlling. So she learned to let go. To trust. There was a lesson in everyone. For her. For her heart. And god, how she had grown to love that part of living.

nothing
that is meant
for your future

will get lost

somewhere in
your past.

i lost
you.

but
i found
me.

so i win.

It took me years to get to this place. To where I can laugh at myself. Smile at my reflection. Love my imperfections. To a place where I can quiet that voice in my head telling me all the things I need to do better. Do more of. Do less of. And arrive at a place where I can hear my heart whispering I'm good enough. Right now. Just as I am. It took me years to stop comparing myself to other people. To their milestones and accomplishments and journeys. To stop wondering when and how and what if. And just enjoy my journey. *Mine.* Unique and long and winding as it may be. So darling, if you don't see me and smile—if you aren't proud of who I am and want to walk beside me—then you can do the best thing for both of us. Keep walking. Because the best me needs someone who loves me for who I am. Now. Completely. Totally. It took me years to get here. To this place where I finally love me. And I can't spend that much time trying to convince someone else they should too. Walk beside me and hold my hand. Or love me enough to walk away.

she was waiting
for the
before — you
and after — you line.
the one
that marked
the beginning.

She was going to wait. They told her to stop believing in fairy tales. And they told her *that* kind of love didn't exist. But she knew they were wrong. She knew *that* kind of love was out there. For her. For each of us. The kind that changed everything—was everything. She heard them tell her to be realistic. To settle down. To stop waiting. But she wouldn't listen. She couldn't. She knew it was out there. The kind of love that drew a before and after line. And because she knew that, simply nothing else would do. So yes, she was going to wait. Even if it took *so* much longer than she'd hoped it would. Because sometimes you just have to get out there and chase the fairy tale. Even if you have to write as you go.

She knew she was going to love a lot of hearts in this lifetime. And she also knew some of them—most of them—were going to break her heart. Maybe a little, maybe a lot. Hell, there were going to be a few, if she was lucky, that ripped the whole damn thing out of her chest and walked away with it. Yes, you heard me. *If she was lucky.* Sounds crazy, right? But she wanted that kind of love. The kind that had the power to break her—even if only for a season. Because that was the *real* kind. The kind that let her know she put it all out there. And she was more than willing to put up with the risk—the healing—that could be the result. She was young enough to still believe and old enough to know how to play the game. She was experienced enough to weed out the ones destined to hurt her and open enough to let people still surprise her. So yes, she was willing to take the shot. Open to playing the odds. And maybe it was because she finally knew her own heart. She wasn't looking for someone to save her. And she didn't need someone to complete her. She just wanted the one who couldn't imagine a better place to wait for tomorrow. Two hearts that face the world together. And laugh like crazy. Yes. She knew her own heart—and that had made all the difference. She knew there were going to be more than a few sparks that burned out between her heart and theirs—and that was ok. She didn't need the light from someone else to lead the way. She had her own fire. And that light was going to lead her wherever this world has destined for her to go.

You love her. I know you do. You love her in the kind of way that makes you want to walk ahead—watching vigilantly for anything and everything that could possibly hurt her. You want to hold her back—behind you—so you can clear the way in front of her. Of the obstacles. Of the danger. Of the dark souls and broken hearts trying to latch on to a beautiful, pure soul like hers. Darling, you love her like you've never loved someone before—but you're doing it wrong. You mean well, I know. But please don't hold her back—push her forward. Arm her with the insight and knowledge and courage to face what comes at her in this life. Whatever it may be. Give her your heart and your hand when she's scared. But don't let her believe—for even one second—that she can't do it on her own. That she isn't the strongest, most capable girl in the whole world. You give her roots. The kind of roots that shows her she has wings. And then you love her enough to let her fly, darling. Even if that means you're not right there by her side. Let her dance out into this world—and touch every part of it. So she knows the beautiful chaos—the yin and yang—the darkness and light. Love her enough—to let her *lead*.

It's not mean. It's not rude. Sometimes you have to do it in your life, sweet girl. You have to choose—yes, choose—who you let in. And no, I don't just mean who you spend time with. Because I know that's not always something you have control of. What I mean is—you have to *choose* who you let *affect* you. Truth is, some people are just plain toxic. They are. They're negative. Draining. They crash into your good days and your happy days and your regular days—and they try to rob you of your joy. Your happiness. Your hope. Maybe you work with them. Maybe you call them family. Or maybe they are just some random person you cross paths with. Whatever the case may be, sometimes you can choose to remove these people from your life. And sometimes you can't. So the trick is to limit their power. There are always two kinds of people in this world. The ones who drain you. And the ones who recharge you. And the trick is how you use these people in your life. When it comes to the ones who drain you—just try to be patient with them, ok? Chances are, you'll have a few you'll never be able to untangle from completely. So put a lot out there for them. Love. Acceptance. Patience. Just don't let any of their negativity flow back towards you, sweet soul. Limit their power. And when it comes to the ones who recharge you? *Gravitate* towards them. They are the fuel of your life. Let them be everywhere. Let them counteract the effect of the ones who drain you. Because it's a beautiful, crazy equation—this life. The positive. The negative. Some people take a little of us, but others hand it back.

don't let her
believe
for even

one second

that she isn't
the strongest,
most capable

girl

in all the
world.

I know you think about it a lot. Those thoughts about the future. And what life is—and you are—going to be one day. The people who love you have dreams for you. You have dreams for yourself. And the universe has plans. Plans that *no one*, including you, could ever imagine in your wildest dreams. Every day you're working towards it. Your eyes see more. Your heart knows more. Your feet are more certain and sure in their steps. And there you are, chasing the good school and the good job and the promotion at the good job. You're studying and planning. You get up early and stay up late. You counsel and advise yourself when you're all alone. You tell yourself what you shouldn't have said, should or shouldn't have done, and will do better next time. You're this beautiful, masterful work in progress, aren't you? You're working *on everything*. The body. The heart. The mind. The soul. And you hear all the things you are doing or need to be doing every day. But you know, what you might not hear—from others or even your own voice—is that you're *ok right now*, too. Even while you're on this journey to be someone—anyone—everything. Darling, you are perfectly amazing. And if you don't take one more step towards this life—this you—you're chasing? That would still be alright. It would. So how about you add that to the things you tell yourself? While you're going through the list at night, replaying the past and the present and planning for the future, try it. Let yourself move forward. Dream. But give yourself permission to do it accepting this you. The draft. The not-quite-there you. The don't-have-it-all-together person who will always dream of being better. Yes. Love that person, too. That's the original. The first edition. And maybe? The absolute best.

She started out with a soft heart. She felt things.

She let in the joy and the sadness. She celebrated and wept with the hearts that crossed her path. And she ended up carrying a bit of their hearts with her. *She loved that.* Her eyes sparkled with hope when she looked at this old world. And her heart whispered to her—told her—that no matter what happened, there was *always* a reason to be happy. To believe. To dream. So she did. And yet somewhere along the way, people started to tell her the world wasn't what she knew. Or imagined. Or dreamt of. They told her it was hard, and cold. That it was full of hate and impossibilities and loss. And she wasn't naive. She could see what the world was, if that was what she chose to look at. But it wasn't. So she turned off the news and the reality shows, and she looked *at people.* At random strangers on the street who changed each other's lives. In small ways or vast ways. Knowingly or unknowingly. She watched the love of families. And hearts who had truly found their soulmates. She watched the gentle clasp of hands that held on after decades of marriage. And the simple, pure laughter of children. She saw the love of mothers and fathers for their children. The young soul who turned their life around, and the old soul who found the courage to start over. She smiles when, as simple as it is, someone holds the door. She knew the world. It wasn't the hard, cold, awful place so many had painted it. She saw the brushstrokes of beauty each and every day. So she would keep her soft heart. And she knew it was all about that choice. For each of us. So she chose *to believe.*

oh, darling.
when it's
right for you,
you will know.
trust me.
you will know.

It's time to do this. I know you've been waiting for the right time. To get through these couple days or weeks or months. To finish something. To start something. But trust me, sweet soul, there is always going to be something on your list. Something that makes you want to wait. Maybe you're scared. Maybe you have no idea if you can actually do it. Maybe you think you're not strong enough yet—that you need more time. *You don't.* Get out there. Tell them how you feel. Walk away. Submit the application. Get on the plane. Start training. Say you're sorry. Darling, whatever it is. *Just do it.* Stop waiting. Stop planning. You're never going to arrive at a time when the universe stops its crazy spinning. And tells you that it's time. So you've got to jump into the driver's seat—pump up the volume—and take control of your own destiny. You are *so* ready. And darling, you've *been* ready. Let's do this.

Darkness scared most people. But not her. She wasn't afraid of what she didn't know. And couldn't see. That girl was forged in the darkness. But she had lived in the light. And she learned long ago that one of two things happens when the world gets dark. She could get lost. Or she could *learn how to see*. The choice was hers. It always had been. But to her, it was never really a choice. Because she wasn't a get-lost kind of girl. She got out there. In the darkness. And she taught herself to see. It was that simple. Because after that, the dark times weren't quite so powerful. They couldn't control her. Make her withdraw. Make her fear the things she didn't know. Her eyes taught her the truth. Darkness didn't mean that good things weren't still there. It just meant she would have to look for them a little differently. And she did. She learned to carry the light with her. And be her own light. She used that fire within her to light her own way—and the way of so many around her. She wasn't afraid. She wasn't unhappy. She wasn't impatient. She knew the truth. The light would be back. It always came back. And until then, she was going to let her heart lead her. It knew the way. Darkness or light—it *always* knew the way.

learn to
forgive yourself
for all the things
you did
when love
was leading you.

Her eyes. They had taken in the world. And explained it to her. They'd shown her seasons changing. And people changing. She'd seen landscapes and trends and entire cities altered. Those eyes had taken her places when she first wanted to be free. And led her home again when she wanted to be loved. She'd watched the people around her grow older and taller and more sure of themselves. Finish school. Find their way. And then *there was her*. She'd been growing and changing and finding herself too. She'd lost things. And been lost. She'd celebrated milestones and friendships. She'd known heartbreak. And love. And both peace and regret. Yes, she'd known a little bit of it all by now. And along the way, her eyes had still been searching. Searching for that one piece or person or accomplishment that would make it all make sense. That would complete the puzzle. She thought it would be profound—*that thing*. She thought she'd stumble upon it and it would change everything. But it was quiet. One morning she just woke up and things were right. Not because everything made sense. Not because she had everything she wanted. But because she finally knew who she was. She was strong enough to fight for what she wanted. And she was smart enough to know what battles to fight. She was experienced enough to cast aside worry. Especially for the things she couldn't change. But most of all, she was forgiving enough to really love herself. That girl used those eyes to see. And all around her—her life was completely different. She *had* and *was* and *wanted to be* something so much more than she thought she'd always wanted to be. But somehow, all was right with the world. And she knew it. She was—finally—who she was *meant* to be. For the very first time.

darling,
no matter
what you do

just never

never

lose your
fire.

Life. What a beautiful, messy, wonderful, painful, joyful mix of opportunity. And Luck. And hard work. And decision. And maybe even a little destiny. And you know, none of us gets the easy road. Despite how it may appear. Every single one of us is fighting *back*, *against*, and *for* something. Something everyone else will know nothing about. We are all struggling with whether we made the right decision. At the right time. And we all want to change things. We have that one moment we wish we could go back and have again. Or the one person we wish things had been different with. And the truth is, *no matter what we think*—we're not all that different from one another. Because life is hard. And confusing. And no one has the big picture all mapped out. No one has all the answers. So we're all just hoping, as we navigate this life—that we're doing it right. That our mistakes teach us. That our loss reminds us. That our hurt strengthens us. And that our hearts carry us. Know this with every part of who you are. In *every* chamber of your heart and in the very depths of your soul. You're going to be ok. Your life is going to turn out exactly and precisely as it should. You will never know what your road is going to look like—but rest assured, darling—it will be yours. And it will take you directly to the *people* you need. And the *experiences* you need. And the life you never knew you always wanted. And it won't be easy. But the end will be worth it. So amidst the unknown, and in the middle of chaos and uncertainty—*please* hang on. Hang on to hope. And keep believing. No matter what you're walking through at this moment, hang on. Let them see you. Bent. Broken. Hurt. Alone. Lost. And then let them call you the one who never—never—stopped hoping.

oh, don't be
afraid.
this is just
the part
where you
find out
who you are.

Don't worry. You won't deter her. She's going to find her happiness. But she's not going to find it where you might think. It won't be when she fixes what's broken. And it won't be when she finds what she lost. She's not waiting until it all works out. And she's not looking for someone else to hand it to her. That girl—she's going to find it *within* her. And then she's going to make it. Totally, completely, and fully. She will teach herself to create her own happiness—so no one can ever control her supply. She knows she's never going to find the world she's looking for. People will never treat her the way they should. And things might never be *just* right. So she's going to get out there and create the world she wants to be part of. A happy one. One that she grows right under her own two feet.

They used to mistake her kindness for weakness.

And that's ok. Because what fuels her soul is so much stronger than whatever they want to believe about her. And what propels her heart forward is so much greater than what holds it back. That girl is a survivor. A warrior. She knows how the world works. She knows we all eat some lies when our hearts are hungry. And we all stumble a bit in the darkness. But she chooses something different for her. For her life. She's not naive. She isn't an idealist. *She's focused.* And she knows the world will respond to the energy she puts out into it. So she focuses on light. And she hopes. And dreams. And she truly still believes that all things are possible. That she will find the heart she is meant to love. And she will become the woman she is meant to be. That girl is unbreakable. She wakes up every single morning and turns off her phone. The news. Social media. And she remembers. What she's working towards. What she wants. What she has *always* wanted. The world will tell her it's impossible. And she's crazy. And it will throw things in her path—trying to make her stumble. But she won't. Because she was born with a heart that was strong enough to fight. And when the world makes her choose, she does. *To believe.*

this
is the year
she **makes** it.

the end.

All around you, it's happening. Hearts are finding each other. Choosing each other. Holding on like hell to each other. And you smile. For real. And you cheer for the ones around you who have found that true, honest, deep, and amazing kind of love. The kind you want, too. The kind your heart whispers to you about. Questions you about. When will it be my turn? When will I find the one that's been searching for me as long as I've been searching for them? When, and how, and where will I find them? And maybe—after all those hard questions—that's the point where you start analyzing. Saying it's never going to happen to you. That it's taking too long. And maybe you start to accept that's not the life you were meant for. But here's the truth, sweet soul. All those questions—they have an answer. And the answer is—your time is coming. It is. But your timeline is not going to be the same as those around you. And you're not going to be able to rush it. Or push it. Or coerce it to happen on the timeline you want it to. Things are coming together. In the way and the order they need to. For your life. And this is the time you need to have faith. And you need to keep putting yourself out there. Throwing your heart and your soul out into the world. Because darling, you will be someone's greatest adventure. You will. They are looking for you just as hard as you are looking for them. So keep going. Keep loving. And keep believing. Until the day you find each other.

She seemed to dance through this life. Unaffected by everything the universe could throw at her. Things that were meant to break her just strengthened her. Things meant to deter her just pushed her further. Loss somehow ended up allowing her to open more doors. She wasn't the kind of girl who looked longingly at the past. She just kept walking. Knowing her journey would be full of amazing things. If she kept her heart open and her eyes clear. She was the kind of girl the world thought had no troubles. Because she smiled. And found joy. Everywhere. And in everything. Truth was—she had plenty of troubles. But she had learned that things like that didn't define her. She had scars. But she just considered them proof she had showed up. She spread her sunshine far and wide. Not because she had everything. But because she thought life was beautiful. *Still.* With all its chaos and uncertainty and twists and turns. She was *that girl.* The one who opened doors. And hearts.

i'll *tell* you
what happened.

you told her
to get out there
and find her life.

so she did.

This is the new me. Yes, I know I'm different—that's *kind* of the point.

I am not going to be the same girl I was. I'm not going to sound the same or be the same or want the same things. It's simple. It's because *I'm not* the same. It's crazy how we look at life—and we all generally agree—that it is this constantly changing, ever-evolving experiment. We all accept that change happens every day—what we want to be, how we want to get there, what we want along the way. It's perfectly fine and completely normal for us to change. And yet, when the people around us start to do it, for some reason, we just can't seem to process it. We can't *accept* it. We ask them *what's wrong,* and we tell them *they're so different now.* Now. That's the part that gets me. Like being different is somehow wrong. Well, I've stopped listening to that. Yes, I'm different now. I've learned a hell of a lot about this girl—and it's been hard-earned. So maybe that means now I've found my voice. Maybe that means I'm not going to be walked on. Actually, that's exactly what that means. I'm not going to waste my time. On things that don't matter. On people that don't matter. And on the pieces of my life that don't get me closer to who I want to be. I've finally learned that it's not about quantity. I've stopped needing the *amount* of everything. Now? Now I want *the good stuff.* The best friends. The beautiful, deep, meaningful connections. The *laugh-til-you-cry* kind of stories. I want *the living.* So yes, I'm different. And let me help you define what that means. *I know who I am now.* And this is exactly who I'm meant to be. I hope you like me. But if you don't? That's ok—I'm not looking for your approval. I'm not that girl anymore.

this
is about
your journey,
sweet girl.

they

don't have
to understand.

*let's
just call
this little detour*

an opportunity.

Sure. It's not the life you planned. Maybe the timing seems off. Things aren't happening like you think they're supposed to. You lost people and things you thought should have stayed. And kept people you'd never thought would be there for a lifetime. You have chased dreams. And goals. All the things you thought you wanted. Or should want. Only to find, looking back, that the random tangents in your life—the haphazard serendipitous moments—were often what changed everything. So maybe your plan for your life is only part of it. Maybe there is a plan much greater for you. That you'll never know the totality of at one time. Something that the universe holds close, and reveals in beautiful, random opportunities. Maybe it looks like everything is being taken from you. But the other way to look at it is better. In those moments when it feels like everything is wrong, consider this. Things are just being reorganized. Regrouped. Reconfigured. And when all the pieces land in the right place, you're going to be ready. For what's next. And if you hadn't had all that, it just wouldn't—couldn't—have worked. Because now your eyes are open. Clear. Ready to see. And you can understand—and accept—and be excited about—what's been laid out before you. The little detour. That you never wanted. But that is going to take you exactly where you never knew you always wanted to be.

The longer she lived, the more and more her perspective on beauty changed. It used to be about clothes. And hair. And shoes. It used to be about all those things other people could *see*. And assess. And envy, just a little. But now? Now it was about something completely different. When she saw beauty in others, it seemed to stem from some inner source. Some place deep within them. A place that manufactured that part of people that just can't be concretely defined. Beauty came from *that*. It was the people she met, and knew, and loved—who were kind. And honest. People who didn't judge others. Or break them down. The ones who weren't too busy to admire the simple, most human interactions. Empathy. Hope. Kindness. But mostly, she noticed the people who still looked at the world with a little bit of magic. With sparkly eyes and real smiles. The ones who still hung on to hope. And goodness. The ones who knew not everyone was going to stand beside them—but reached out their hands anyway. She'd met a lot of these beautiful people. And she knew it wasn't likely she'd see any of them on the cover of some magazine. Because you can't take a picture of that kind of beauty. You can only *live* it. And *feel* it. And *be* it.

She wouldn't lie to you. Her heart was whole now, but it hadn't always been. She had worn it on her sleeve, and it had been stepped on a few times. She had handed it—with hope and trust and starry eyes— to a few someones along the way to protect. There had been times when she'd said *those three words* out loud—and silence had echoed back. And so each and every time, that girl left a piece or two of that whole heart she started with behind. Sometimes, simply because it hurt too much to go back and retrieve it. And others, because it just kind of seemed some pieces belonged with the ones who took them. Maybe that was just part of it—they built that love in her, and it was theirs to take with them. But either way, minus those pieces, that heart of hers was not broken. It was not empty and not hurt. No. That heart of hers was—is—still quite amazingly whole. Because that's who she is. And that's what hearts do. Each time hers broke, she glued it back together. She picked up the pieces and she figured out how to weave those threads into something new. Into something that kept working and kept growing. Something that—through its holes and bruises and little cracks—somehow, got stronger each time. Not with walls. Or an impenetrable fortress. Just stronger. Because she learned the universe has all kinds of love. And the kind where she learns to love herself and her life and all the people and moments in it—that love does a lot to fill in the holes left behind by the starry-eyed heartbreak kind. So yes, she has loved. And been loved. And has lost, and been lost. But you know, she has also *learned*. She has learned how to survive. And more than that, how to love. By the only means one can ever really learn how to love. By loving.

It took more years than she wanted to admit to get here. But maybe it wasn't so much about the process as it was the destination. Less the fact that it took some time—more about the fact she never gave up until she was standing here. *Happily.* In her own skin. And even still, she didn't get here because suddenly she was everything the world always wanted her to be. Polished like the airbrushed models in magazines. Wearing the perfect clothes. Able to charm any room, and handle any situation. No, that wasn't her. She was far from perfect—inside or out. She had made buckets of mistakes. And she continued to. She had parts of her she'd always wished were different. But I guess after all that wishing and wanting, she finally just came to this place of contentment. Of peace. She was never going to be that idea of perfection the world had painted for her. And that was perfectly fine with her—because that's no longer who she wanted to be. This girl she had met—this best version of herself— was someone she was really proud of. She was beautiful because she was comfortable in her own skin. She was confident in what she had—and also what she didn't. She was somehow *graceful* in how she walked through life. Even if she tripped over a few sidewalk cracks along the way. She was quiet, yet well-spoken, because she knew what she had to say. Her voice had matured. And now it was connected to her heart—not her brain. She liked this version of herself. And she knew it was only going to get better from here. She accepted that she was going to love a lot of hearts along the way. But there was only one person she was going to spend her life with. Herself. So she spent a little more time learning about that girl. And you know what? She fell in love.

*just remember,
not all change
feels positive
in the beginning.*

Maybe you think you broke her just because you stole her smile for a little while. You didn't. And you won't. When you walked away, you thought you'd won. You thought you'd won because she loved you more than you loved her—and that just wasn't enough for you. When you walked away that last time—sent that last text—had that last call—you thought you'd had the last word. The best argument. You were content because you were right—and she wasn't—and it ended, just like you knew it would. And so when you imagine her now, she's still crying by the phone. Loving you. Wishing you'd call. Thinking you're the *best* and *only* person she can ever be with. You see her, drowning, in that puddle of self-doubt you tried so hard to build into her. Well, *stop*. And let me clarify a few things for you. First of all, she's not there, waiting by the phone. She no longer thinks about all those good times you had, wondering if you're ever going to come back. Actually, she *hardly* thinks of you at all. When you stopped loving her, something happened to her alright. Something huge. That's actually the one—*one*—thing she credits you with. You taught her to love herself enough to know when someone wasn't loving her enough. And that is exactly what she needed. To finally—finally—start loving herself. So hey—you didn't break her, darling. She wouldn't give you that power. That girl loved you in a way you're never going to find again but are always going to look for. And trust me, *you will* look for it. But as for her? She's not the same girl she was. She is strong and independent and confident. She is open and loving and free. So, when you think of her (and I know you will), just know this: you never broke her. The only thing you did was push her to the edge. Like, *right* to the edge. But she didn't jump, darling. *She flew.*

That girl. Let me tell you about who she is. She's this beautiful, amazing work in progress. Somehow perfect in who she is today and yet always on her way to something greater. And she *changes* things. *God, does she ever change things.* She walks through this life and makes people notice her. But not because she asks for it. They just do. People stop and watch her—they watch the certainty she walks with. The elegance. The class. They observe the kindness she shows others. She's this beautiful soul who somehow lights the darkness. And shows the world there is still good. She steals moments that change lifetimes and she starts ripples that effect change. She wants to be remembered as a spark. Someone who can start things that change everything. Who can make this crazy old world better. And people stronger. And life happier. She wants to *believe.* She knows she doesn't have all the answers and accepts she never will. But she has contentment and calm in her heart. Because she trusts the timing and blessings of what this life has planned for her. And while she's waiting to see what is in store, she's out there. Opening doors, holding hands, and touching hearts. It's just who she is.

she had
found her voice.
finally.

She always had wings. You just taught her how to use them. And maybe that's what it was all about, darling. Your little piece of her world. Maybe you were made to love her less than she deserved. And maybe that simple lesson taught her the most important one of all. How to love *herself.* And you know, she'll take the heartbreak if that's the lesson. Just don't come back to the same place you left her. She has wings now. And she won't be there.

I know—you want to *know*, right? You want to know when and how and where. You thrive on those details. You always have. You like to know things—to plan—to be able to expect what's coming. And be prepared. And that's why this chapter has been the hardest for you. Because there are more things you don't know than things you do. More questions than answers. More loose ends than ends that have been tied up nicely by the forces of the universe. Oh, darling—I think you need to rename this chapter of your life. Right now you think it's just a quiet chapter—one where nothing extraordinarily good or bad happens. Ok, well that's good too. But how about you look at it as your *balance chapter.* Your rebuilding chapter. The one that strengthens you without the storms raging around you. The one that gives you enough time to think—about all those things that have happened and are happening and might happen. Darling, why don't you just let this be the time of untying? You have a lot of knots from those last few chapters, don't you? So rather than figuring out what's coming next—and when—how about you just focus on *you*? And making sure you can stand tall and walk straight into a future you deserve—and are ready for—without those knots pulling you back into a past you no longer belong in. It's alright to live this part without knowing, sweet soul. Because this is just the middle. It's most definitely not the end.

You did more than you think. More than you were supposed to do with your one chapter of her book. She loved you and you didn't love her—she stayed and you walked away. And then there was the fact that you stayed whole and she broke. Broke into millions of pieces that cut like daggers. Pieces that taught her how much souls can hurt each other in this world. So yes, that was supposed to be your chapter. That one great heartbreak that started with starry-eyed love and ended without a good-bye. The next chapter—the one where she taught herself to heal—to walk on her own two feet—and to trust again? That was supposed to *be hers*. Your chapter was supposed to end with that last bit of silence on that last page. But it didn't. She let you bleed over into the next chapter—which she normally doesn't let herself do. She lets you—well, the *theoretical* you, because there's no way you're ever getting back into her world—affect her still. But not in the way you thought. She's not broken anymore. She's not waiting by the phone. She's not weak or helpless or hurting. No—you broke her, but when you did—it awakened something in her. Something big. Something that started as a spark and rages now as a wildfire. Something that knows what to chase and what it wants. It's like she is living—breathing—tasting this life for the first time. And you did that. Somehow, let her find what made her whole by shattering her heart into a million pieces first. I guess that's sometimes how it works. The only way we can see the things we need to see—when we can't hide behind our image of having it all together. So yes. Thank you. For your little part in her story. You may have hurt her with your smile and your broken soul—hurt her like she's never been hurt before—but you awakened something in her, too. *And it's hungry.*

The day dawned. And she could think of yesterday.

Of her mistakes. Of her *should-haves* and *could-haves* and *might-have-beens*. She could focus on the people who have hurt her. Stood in her way. Taken her time. She could focus on scars and bruises and falls. But she doesn't. And she won't. Because she looks at each day as new. A blank canvas. A clean slate. An unwritten page. And she begins each day with an open heart. And clear eyes. She's not bitter or hateful. She doesn't hold back. And she doesn't need time. She's focused on life. And living. And being happy. And although she's strong enough to carry yesterday, she doesn't. She saves her strength for today. For tomorrow. And she smiles. Ready to face what the world has in store for her. Ready for the next chapter. No matter how her story began. She is ready. Ready, for this next amazing opportunity to completely change how her story is going to end.

but
i don't
drown.

i rise.

Here's the thing about chapters. When you're writing them, you tend to get too close. Your perspective becomes about *detail*. About how just those few pages play out. How they start and end. And a little bit about what happens in the middle. And you start to think that those few pages—those few people and experiences and stories that star in that one chapter—have the power to alter everything. And maybe in some ways they do. But not like you'd think. You're going to think when you're in the middle of a chapter that everything needs to be fixed by the end. That all your questions need answers and all the ends need beginnings and all the people need to stay. Darling, they don't. And truth? *They won't.* Because here's the thing. This is— just—a piece of your story. It's not your story. And this part that you're writing now—even though every single part of you may be getting lost in the details of this one chapter—is going to work out. It is. But you're going to need to give it time to fit. And you're going to need to keep writing. And most importantly, you're going to need to trust yourself. Because you're the author. And you choose what happens after this part. Write people in, or write them out. Change your direction or your mind. Make things right. Go back. Move forward. Darling—do what you need to do. And that's the beautiful part about it. You can change everything. Or nothing. Yes, you made a mistake. Or had wild success. You lost something you can't even fathom living without. You loved someone. Your heart was broken. You trusted the wrong person. Or the right one. You were careless or hurtful or wrong. You were happy or wild or free. Yes, that is *life*. And it's beautiful how the pieces start to fit. But that was a chapter. And this is a book. And darling, what you do with it now is what defines your story. Write it well, sweet soul. Write it well.

Call to Action

Thank you for finding this book. And reading it. And making it *all* the way here to the last few pages. And thank you *even more* for taking this journey—for being open to something different—for allowing me to join you on those first few beautifully hard steps. I hope you've come through this book with a heart that's a little stronger. A little surer. Maybe—just one that is full of a little more hope for tomorrow. And darling? Just know that it's a long journey back to your own heart. And it takes time. Go easy on yourself, sweet soul. Go easy.

And just so you know, there is so much more where this came from. I write these letters every day. And I post them out there in the hopes that they will find the heart that is looking for them. So please join me. On the journey. Visit @liveinthedetails on Instagram, Facebook, and Tumblr.

Acknowledgements

There are so many hearts that made this book possible. I know that in writing this, I am inevitably (and unintentionally) going to forget some of the beautiful souls who were a part of this incredible journey. Please know that—truly—a writer soaks up inspiration from every single person that dances into their lives and every single experience they do—and don't—want to have. I know I could never thank you all the right way. But I'm going to try.

First and foremost, I want to thank my family for their tireless and boundless support of this lifelong dream. You were the ones who listened. Who believed. Who watched me write hundreds of stories with pink pens on elementary school paper. Who fought for me and stood up for me. Who heard me say from the time I was eight years old that one day I was going to be a writer. And one day, I was going to publish a book. And yes, the big dream—that *one day,* I was going to change the world. And so because—*because*—of you, *we* just may do it.

Second, and equally as important—I want to thank my beautiful friend Rachel for sitting with me at a coffee shop on a snowy January night and reminding me who I was. You were the one who asked me to stop being *so busy* and start getting focused. And you—*you*—were the one that I credit with creating *Live in the Details.* You told me to get back to my writing and put it out there for the world to see. And because I did, you gave me a platform to touch this world through my words. Thank you from the absolute bottom of my heart for making me believe in myself again. And for giving me the platform I needed to be the change I want to be in this world.

I tend to think it's not just the people who love us that change our lives for the better. Sometimes—often—it's the people who break us, too. The ones we sometimes want to go back in time and redo. So, this one goes unnamed—but he knows who he is. When we look back, I think we tend to get all the answers we need in place of all the questions we've asked along the way. So—I know now that the reason you were in my life was to break me. Break me so that I could start over and rebuild myself into the person I *always* knew I *always* wanted to be. And darling, just so you know—I am so totally whole now. So thank you for not loving me enough. And for causing the heartbreak that let me find the greatest love story of my life. *Mine.*

The rest of my thank-yous—truly, are to the following beautiful souls who helped me bring *Courage to Rise* to life:

My publisher, Morgan James.

My oh-so-talented editor, Katherine Rawson.

The beautiful photographers who generously and selflessly donated their talent to the world via *www.unsplash.com* and *www.pixabay.com.*

The community of amazingly strong, amazingly supportive souls on *Live in the Details* who change me every single day—who build me up and make me smile and mostly, who let me live my dream. You are the reason this is all possible. As a writer, ironically, I truly have no words for what you've been able to do for my heart.

And lastly, because I always joked I would—I want to thank my third-grade teacher. She apparently told my parents at the lovely age of eight that I couldn't write. And I should find another dream. Well, this book is for you. Not out of spite or sarcasm—but truthfully, out of gratitude. Sometimes the people who tell us no don't cause the fire to smolder. Sometimes—they cause it to *rage.*

And so she did.

***

I would like to thank the group of incredibly talented, wonderfully selfless photographers who so willingly donate their beautiful works of art to the world via Unsplash.com and Pixabay.com. You guys are amazing. Keep making this world a more beautiful place.

And a special thanks to the following beautiful souls, whose works appear in this book:

Amanda Bear, Andrew Neel, Becca Tapert, Benjamin Davies, Brian Mann, Brigitte Tohm, Brooke Cagle, Bruce Christianson, Caleb Jones, Christopher Campbell, Cody Black, Colin Maynard, Cristina Gottardi, Daiga Ellaby, Daniel Jensen, David Moum, Demetrius Washington, Diego PH, Drew Graham, Everton Vila, Gabriele Ribeiro, Jakob Owens, Jason Long, Jessica Polar, João Silas, John Reign Abarintos, Jonathan Daniels, Joshua Earle, Joyce Huis, Juan Jose, Jyotirmoy Gupta, Konstantin Kopachinsky, Leio McLaren, Matthew Henry, Megan Savoie, Mink Mingle, Morgan Sessions, Myriam's Photos, Nathan McBride, Nik MacMillan, Pete Bellis, Phuoc Le, Ryan Moreno, Seth Doyle, Szilard Toth, Tamara Menzi, Tanalee Youngblood, Toa Heftiba, Tommy Lisbin, Tony Ross, Tyler Nix, Uroš Jovičić, Utomo Hendra Saputra, Will Swann, Yannis Papanastasopoulos, Yoann Boyer.

About the Author

Emma Grace, who writes under the name *Live in the Details* on Instagram and Facebook, has *always* been in love with words. And it's safe to say—with an audience on Instagram and Facebook approaching two hundred thousand in just two years—that her fans love her words too. She is raw, real, and honest—and seems to capture in a simple and beautiful way all the things that women see and feel and are.

Originally from the Hudson Valley in upstate New York, Emma now lives in Arlington, Virginia, just outside of Washington, DC, with a busy consulting career alongside her writing.

Morgan James
Speakers Group

www.TheMorganJamesSpeakersGroup.com

We connect Morgan James published authors with live and online events and audiences who will benefit from their expertise.

Morgan James makes all of our titles available
through the Library for All Charity Organization.

www.LibraryForAll.org